Contents

Brain and Body in Sport and Exercise

Brain and Body in Sport and Exercise

Biofeedback Applications in Performance Enhancement

Edited by

Boris Blumenstein
Wingate Institute for Physical Education and Sport, Israel

Michael Bar-Eli
Ben-Gurion University of the Negev, Beer-Sheva; and Wingate Institute for Physical Education and Sport, Israel

Gershon Tenenbaum
Florida State University, USA

JOHN WILEY & SONS, LTD

Baffins Lane, Chichester,
West Sussex PO19 1UD, UK

National 01243 779777
International (+44) 1243 779777
e-mail (for orders and customer service enquiries): cs-books@wiley.co.uk
Visit our Home Page on: http://www.wiley.co.uk or http://www.wiley.com

Other Wiley Editorial Offices

John Wiley & Sons, Inc., 605 Third Avenue,
New York, NY 10158-0012, USA

WILEY-VCH Verlag GmbH, Pappelallee 3,
D-69469 Weinheim, Germany

John Wiley & Sons Australia, Ltd., 33 Park Road, Milton,
Queensland 4064, Australia

John Wiley & Sons (Asia) Pte, Ltd., 2 Clementi Loop #02-01,
Jin Xing Distripark, Singapore 129809

John Wiley & Sons (Canada), Ltd., 22 Worcester Road,
Rexdale, Ontario M9W 1L1, Canada

British Library Cataloguing in Publication Data

A catalogue record for this book is available from the British Library

ISBN 0-471-49906-4 (cased)
ISBN 0-471-49907-2 (paper)

Typeset in 10/12pt Times from the author's disks by TechBooks, New Delhi, India
Printed and bound in Great Britain by Biddles Ltd., Guildford and King's Lynn
This book is printed on acid-free paper responsibly manufactured from sustainable forestry, in which at least two trees are planted for each one used for paper production.

About the Editors

Boris Blumenstein is the Head of the Sport Psychology Section and Biofeedback Laboratory at the Ribstein Center for Sport Medicine Sciences and Research, Wingate Institute, Netanya, Israel. He received his Ph.D. in sport psychology in 1980 from the All Union Institute for Research in Sport, Department of sport psychology, Moscow, Russia (formerly the USSR). His extensive experience in sport psychology spans some 25 years, culminating in applied work at the elite level. He has been the sport psychologist consultant and advisor to the Soviet national and Olympic teams and since 1990 to the Israeli national and Olympic teams (including the delegations to Atlanta, 1996, and Sydney, 2000). He is author of over 60 refereed journal articles and book chapters, mainly in the area of sport and exercise psychology. He has also presented more than 40 scientific works at international and national conferences and workshops. His current research interests include mental skills training for performance, stress–performance relationship, and effectiveness of different mental interventions (biofeedback, music, imagery, VCR) in athletic competition readiness. He is currently president of the Israeli Society for Sport Psychology and Sociology and a representative within the European Federation of Sport Psychology (FEPSAC).

Michael Bar-Eli is an Associate Professor in the Department of Business Administration, School of Management, Ben-Gurion University of the Negev, Beer-Sheva; and Senior Researcher at the Ribstein Center for Sport Medicine Sciences and Research, Wingate Institute, Netanya, Israel. He studied psychology and sociology in Israel and sport psychology and sociology in the German Sport University, Cologne, from which he received his doctorate magna cum laude. Bar-Eli has published over 90 international refereed journal articles and book chapters, and numerous journal articles, book chapters, and books in Hebrew. He is the current "Social Aspects" section editor of the *International Journal of Sport Psychology* and associate editor of *Psychology of Sport and Exercise*. He served in senior positions in the psychological organs of the Israel Defense Forces and has often acted as psychological consultant to athletes, primarily in team sports. Bar-Eli is past president of the Israeli Society for Sport Psychology and Sociology, current senior vice president of ASPASP (Asian South-Pacific Association of Sport Psychology), and past chairperson of scientific affairs of the managing council of FEPSAC. He served as guest professor at the Norwegian Sport University, Oslo, Norway in 1995.

Gershon Tenenbaum is a Professor of Sport and Exercise Psychology at the Florida State University, College of Education, Department of Educational Research. He was previously in the Department of Psychology at The University of Southern Queensland, Australia, and the Director of the Research and Sport Medicine Center at the Wingate Institute in Israel. A graduate of Tel-Aviv University and the University of Chicago (Ph.D.) in measurement, evaluation, and statistical analysis, he is past president of the International Society of Sport Psychology and the editor of the *International Journal of Sport Psychology*. Professor Tenenbaum has published extensively in the area of methodology and research design in sport and exercise, decision-making and cognition, and, recently, social–cognitive perspectives in perceived exertion and exertion tolerance. He worked together with Boris Blumenstein and Michael Bar-Eli on the methodological developments and implications of biofeedback technique with athletes. His works have been published in books and refereed articles in the psychology, education, sport psychology, and exercise physiology and medicine domains. He is a member of several professional organizations, including the New York Academy of Science, the American Society for the Advancement of Applied Sciences, and the International and American Sport and Exercise Psychology Societies. He is married with three children and two dogs.

About the Authors

Dave Collins holds the Chair of Physical Education and Sport Performance and is Head of Department at the University of Edinburgh. Following earlier careers as a professional soldier and teacher of physical education, he moved to sports psychology in the early 1980s. Professor Collins's work is eclectic but has a common focus on the mechanism through which psychological constructs impact on human behavior. Psychophysiology forms a major focus of this work and is used in ongoing research in association with biochemical kinematic and self-report data. Dave has worked as a sport psychologist in a wide variety of sports. His current work focuses on athletics, judo, and the popular Scottish sport of curling. When not working as an applied sport psychologist or researching, Dave enjoys participation in any sport where his poor levels of co-ordination are not a barrier to success.

With a keen interest in the underlying dynamics of physical activity and competitive sport performance, **Mandy Corbett** completed a Bachelor of Physical Education degree and a Master of Arts degree in psychology at the University of the Witwatersrand, Johannesburg, South Africa. She then went on to complete a Master of Psychology (Sport and Exercise) degree at the University of Southern Queensland, Australia. Following Mandy's return to South Africa, she has been involved in lecturing on sport psychology and biomechanics at the University of the Witwatersrand, providing psychological skills training and counseling to junior African tennis players at the International Tennis Federation Training Centre in Pretoria, as well as writing sport psychology-related articles for a South African tennis newspaper and presenting "mental toughness" tips for tennis players on a national television sports show.

Panteleimon Ekkekakis is an Assistant Professor in the Department of Health and Human Performance at Iowa State University. He received his undergraduate degree from the University of Athens (Greece), his M.S. from Kansas State University, and his Ph.D. from the University of Illinois at Urbana–Champaign. His general area of research is exercise psychology, with emphasis on the affective changes that accompany single bouts of exercise. In particular, Dr. Ekkekakis is interested in the conceptualization and assessment of affect, the dose–response relationship between exercise intensity and affective responses, and the cognitive and interoceptive correlates of these responses. He is an active member of the American College of Sports Medicine and the North American Society for the Psychology of Sport and Physical Activity.

Anastasia Kitsantas earned her Ph.D. in educational psychology from the Graduate School and University Center of the City University of New York. She is an assistant professor of educational psychology, Graduate School of Education, George Mason University, USA. She is the 1997 recipient of the outstanding dissertation award of the American Psychological Association Division 15. Her research interests and teaching focus on social cognitive processes, and self-regulated learning in academic, sports, and health-related settings. Her publications include works on the development of academic, health, and athletic self-regulation, self-regulated strategies, self-efficacy, and peak performance.

Steven J. Petruzzello is an Associate Professor in the Department of Kinesiology at the University of Illinois at Urbana–Champaign. He received his Ph.D. from Arizona State University in 1991 with a specialization in exercise and sport psychology. Professor Petruzzello is currently serving as editor of the *Journal of Sport and Exercise Psychology*. He is an active member of the Society for Psychophysiological Research and the North American Society for the Psychology of Sport and Physical Activity, and is a Fellow in the American College of Sports Medicine. His research interests are in the area of exercise psychology. His work has primarily focused on the examination of the affective/emotional changes resulting from exercise, specifically from a psychophysiological perspective.

Preface

The goal of this book is to introduce the field of applied psychophysiology to sport and physical education—to students, teachers, athletes, coaches, and sport psychologists. It is our aim to familiarize them with biofeedback, a technique that facilitates the self-regulation of arousal states. The relevance of biofeedback interventions to athletic preparation is evident in the "psychophysiological principle" presented by Green, Green, and Walters (1970), which states that every physiological change is accompanied by a parallel change in the mental and emotional state and, conversely, every change in the mental and emotional state, conscious or unconscious, is accompanied by an appropriate change in the physiological state. Thus, biofeedback can be a powerful tool for physiological change, increasing individual awareness and control over the body, and reducing habitual physiological tensions.

The first biofeedback applications were limited to clinical medical practice. In 1968 Joe Kamiya demonstrated that subjects could voluntarily control their brainwaves (Kamiya, 1968), and in 1977 John Basmajian showed that subjects could learn to control single motor units in their spinal cord (Basmajian, 1977). The possibilities offered by biofeedback—i.e., controlling our bodies through brainwaves—seemed quite fascinating at that time. However, biofeedback applications, which became quite popular in the medical area, are still in need of further development in the sport/exercise domain.

Quite a large amount of good biofeedback research has been conducted in sport and exercise, especially during the 1980s and early 1990s. Most studies found positive effects of biofeedback interventions on performance, but usually in laboratory settings. Thus, we agree with the observation of Crews, Lochbaum, and Karoly (2001, p. 578), that "one of the criticisms of biofeedback training has been the ability to transfer the learned response to performance in the real world." In fact, the current state of knowledge on biofeedback applications in sport concerning factors such as methods, number of training sessions, the planning of biofeedback interventions, their place in the regular training process, and mental preparation, is not sufficiently clear. This is because research is conducted mainly in laboratory settings and it is difficult to recruit elite athletes for applied research, as well as being due to technical problems. As a result, most practitioners have insufficient knowledge regarding the psychophysiology of sport and exercise, specifically in the area of biofeedback applications.

Our own experience with biofeedback started upon the initiation of the biofeedback laboratory at Wingate by Gershon Tenenbaum in 1991. Together with Gershon Tenenbaum, we worked for several years on the development of biofeedback research and applications, especially with elite athletes.

During the last decade, we revealed that biofeedback has great possibilities and potential for practical sport, but the methods for biofeedback application in sport are still rather underdeveloped. Generally speaking, biofeedback interventions have not become a part of ordinary mental or physical preparation in sport, and many coaches, athletes, and physical education students do not know about the significant potential of biofeedback for sport and exercise psychology and the training process. Thus, we believe that the idea of presenting the current state of biofeedback applications in sport and exercise would be highly interesting and beneficial to the sport/exercise and physical education public.

This book contains six chapters. Chapter 1, "Biofeedback as Applied Psychophysiology in Sport and Exercise: Conceptual Principles for Research and Practice" (Michael Bar-Eli), presents a framework for psychophysiology and biofeedback applications in sport and exericse. In the remaining chapters an attempt is made to emphasize the link between theory and practice within various specific areas of sport/exercise psychology. Chapter 2 is entitled "Psychophysiology and Athletic Performance" (Dave Collins). This chapter presents definitions and methods in psychophysiology, the relation between physiological measures and sport performance, and some elements of biofeedback systems. Chapter 3 is entitled "Biofeedback Applications in Sport and Exercise: Research Findings" (Boris Blumenstein). The main purpose of this chapter is to discuss the current state of applied biofeedback research in the following areas: biofeedback and the reduction of anxiety, biofeedback and the improvement of muscle performance, and biofeedback and the improvement of athletic performance in different sports. Chapter 4, entitled "Biofeedback Training in Sport" (Boris Blumenstein, Michael Bar-Eli, Dave Collins), describes two examples of current biofeedback training programs applied in different sports, and presents extensive practical material from training and competition, including general, daily, and weekly biofeedback training plans. In Chapter 5, "Biofeedback in Exercise Psychology" (Panteleimon Ekkekakis and Steven Petruzzello), biofeedback research and applications in exercise are described, in particular the relations between biofeedback interventions and mental health and the factors that affect these relations. Chapter 6 is entitled "Biofeedback: Applications and Methodological Concerns" (Gershon Tenenbaum, Mandy Corbett, and Anastasia Kitsantas) and describes methodological aspects of biofeedback application in sport are described, including the relevant limitations and implications for biofeedback training in sport. In a sense, this chapter "closes the circle" of discussion related to conceptual principles introduced in Bar-Eli's chapter (Chapter 1).

This book represents the results of the scientific and applied work of some of the leading experts in biofeedback applications in sport and exercise. Its content is highly relevant, not only for the specialist in sport psychology, but also for practitioners such as athletes, coaches, and physical education teachers and students interested in the area of sport psychophysiology and biofeedback. Thus, we do hope that many of the sport psychology practices presented in this book will be implemented by academicians in the field and practitioners in research, teaching, consultation, and other applications.

BORIS BLUMENSTEIN
MICHAEL BAR-ELI
GERSHON TENENBAUM

REFERENCES

Basmajian, J. V. (1977). Motor learning and control: A working hypothesis. *Archives of Physical Medicine and Rehabilitation*, **58**, 38–41.
Crews, D., Lochbaum, M., & Karoly, P. (2001). Self-regulation: Concepts, methods and strategies in sport and exercise. In R. Singer, H. Hausenblas, & C. Janelle (eds.), *Handbook of sport psychology* (pp. 566–581) (2nd ed.). New York: J. Wiley & Sons.
Green, E., Green, A., & Walters, E. (1970). Voluntary control of internal states: Psychological and physiological. *Journal of Transpersonal Psychology*, **2**, 1–26.
Kamiya, J. (1968). Conscious control of brain waves. *Psychology Today*, **1**, 56–60.

Acknowledgments

Our thanks go to all the contributing authors for their perseverance and patience. Our gratitude is due to Dr Vivien J. Ward and Mrs Helen Ilter, and all the other staff at John Wiley & Sons, Ltd., who helped this book see the light of day. In particular, we would like to emphasize the technical contributions of Ms Dinah Olswang and Dr Yitzhak Weinstein, and their efforts and support during the preparation of this book.

CHAPTER 1

Biofeedback as Applied Psychophysiology in Sport and Exercise: Conceptual Principles for Research and Practice

Michael Bar-Eli

INTRODUCTION

The concept of biofeedback was introduced during the end of the 1960s. Since then, its development has accelerated in many areas (Moss, 1994, 1998). According to Blanchard and Epstein (1978, p. 2), biofeedback is "a process in which a person learns to reliably influence physiological responses of two kinds: either responses which are not ordinarily under voluntary control or responses which ordinarily are easily regulated but for which regulation has broken down", due to some reason (e.g., trauma or disease).

Having such definitions in mind, sport psychology was attracted to biofeedback as early as in the 1980s, with early sport applications of biofeedback being designed to modify athletes' arousal state (e.g., Zaichkowsky, 1983). As applied research in this field started to identify psychophysiological conditions associated with performance enhancement, its emphasis changed substantially towards the study of closed skill (e.g., target) sports (Collins, 1995). However, the issue of biofeedback is still under-researched in the sport-psychological professional practical literature, in particular in an area which is highly relevant to professional practice, namely the use of biofeedback as part of larger multifaceted treatment programs (Blumenstein & Bar-Eli, 2001).

Brain and Body in Sport and Exercise: Biofeedback Applications in Performance Enhancement.
Edited by Boris Blumenstein, Michael Bar-Eli, and Gershon Tenenbaum.

To cope appropriately with this situation, a transactional perspective on biofeedback is required. In what follows, an attempt will be made to further establish and promote this idea.

PSYCHOPHYSIOLOGY AS A STATEMENT ON THE BRAIN–BODY RELATIONSHIP

The brain–body issue has always been a subject of human interest. According to Andreassi (2000), there is evidence that the mutual relationships between body organs, mental events, and human behavior were of interest even for the cavepeople in the Stone Age (i.e., some 250 000 years ago), although the earliest recorded expressions of such an interest may probably be traced back into Egyptian papyri dating from the sixteenth century BCE.

A brief look at the historical development of psychophysiology since its earliest days (Andreassi, 2000) reveals that the main idea of psychophysiology across the ages has been that every physiological change whatsoever is accompanied by a parallel change in the mental and/or emotional state. Green, Green, and Walters (1970, p. 3) have formulated this central psychophysiological principle as follows: "Every change in the physiological state is accompanied by an appropriate change in the mental emotional state, conscious or unconscious, and conversely, every change in the mental emotional state, conscious or unconscious, is accompanied by an appropriate change in the physiological state." Essentially, this statement reflects a very deep, firm view concerning the "eternal" brain–body issue.

Evidently, physical or emotional stress, for example, is associated with various physiological and psychological responses (Neiss, 1988). Elevated heart rate and increased anxiety are two of the most accepted indicators of stress (Raglin, 1992). Falk and Bar-Eli's (1995) literature review indicates that the effects of physical and emotional stress on heart rate response have been investigated among various athletes, such as automobile drivers, racquet ball players, and swimmers, with numerous studies reporting an elevation in heart rate during parachuting; other physiological or psychological facets of parachuting have also been investigated. However, as Falk and Bar-Eli (1995) stated, most of the earlier studies that investigated the response to the stress of parachuting have focused on physiological *or* psychological indices of stress, but, except for a few studies, not on both.

Falk and Bar-Eli (1995) adopted a different approach. More specifically, these researchers examined the psychophysiological stress responses to parachuting using two indicators of stress: heart rate (a physiological index) and state anxiety scores (a psychological index). This approach demonstrates the central idea of the psychophysiological principle, as formulated by Green et al. (1970). However, much more is involved in this simple parachuting example, as we will see below.

PERSON, ENVIRONMENT, TASK: ON THE TRIADIC DETERMINATION OF HUMAN PERFORMANCE

In their seminal work published over 50 years ago, Dewey and Bentley (1949) argued that from an historical perspective, the development of knowledge within scientific disciplines usually follows a systematic, lawful process. According to this idea, objects are first regarded in the discipline as behaving under their own power, a phase of development which is labeled "self-action." Later on, when objects are regarded as being in a causal interrelation of one object acting upon the other, the body of knowledge under consideration is said to be in an "interactional" phase of development. Finally, the scientific discipline develops into the "process transaction" phase, when objects are conceived as relating to one another within an entire system.

Within psychology, it has long been debated as to which source accounts for most of the variance in human behavior (Pervin, 1985). For instance, Ekehammar (1974) differentiated between "personologism" and "situationism." "Personologism" advocates stable, intraorganismic constructs as the main determinants of behavior, whereas "situationism" emphasizes situational factors as the main source of behavioral variance. In 1974, it seemed to Ekehammar that psychology was moving toward being governed by interactionism. The latter "can be regarded as the synthesis of personologism and situationism, which implies that neither the person nor the situation per se is emphasized, but the interaction of these two factors is regarded as the main source of behavioral variation" (p. 1026). Using Dewey and Bentley's (1949) terminology, some investigators have proceeded even further toward transactionism. For example, in line with ideas proposed by earlier leading psychologists such as Cronbach (1957), Pervin (1977) stated that too much psychological research had been conducted on the self-action level and suggested that transactionism had a greater potential for investigating complex human behavior, particularly in applied settings.

According to this approach, in order to adequately analyze a parachutist's performance, for example, at least two different factors should be taken into account, namely the athlete's personal characteristics and the environmental conditions (situation) in which he or she is jumping. However, this person–situation interrelationship can be meaningful for understanding one's performance only if we take into account the task demands under consideration. Thus, performance is conceived as being a function of a person–environment fit (Pervin, 1977), which is determined by the unique demands and requirements of the particular task to be performed.

Essentially, this approach reflects a transactional view of motor performance variability. Such a view has been recommended for sport psychological research in order to increase its ecological validity (Tenenbaum & Bar-Eli, 1995a). More recently, Bandura (1997) recommended a similar approach for general psychology under the label: "the triadic reciprocal causation of human agency" (p. 6). Nitsch and Munzert (1997, p. 117) illustrated the essentials of this person–environment–task transaction in terms of three overlapping circles corresponding to these three performance determinants.

A TRANSACTIONAL MODEL OF HUMAN PERFORMANCE

Taken together with the central psychophysiological principle of Green et al. (1970, p. 3) cited above, the performance (behavior) of athletes (e.g., parachutists) within a transactional system can be conceptualized taking into account the environment (situation) and "the psychophysiological principle", namely the interrelations between the physiological and the mental and emotional components of behavior (see Figure 1.1).

Nitsch and Munzert's (1997) transactional approach emphasizes unique person–environment–task constellations, but mainly in the subjective (as opposed to the objective) sense. Thus, this approach stresses specific combinations of these three

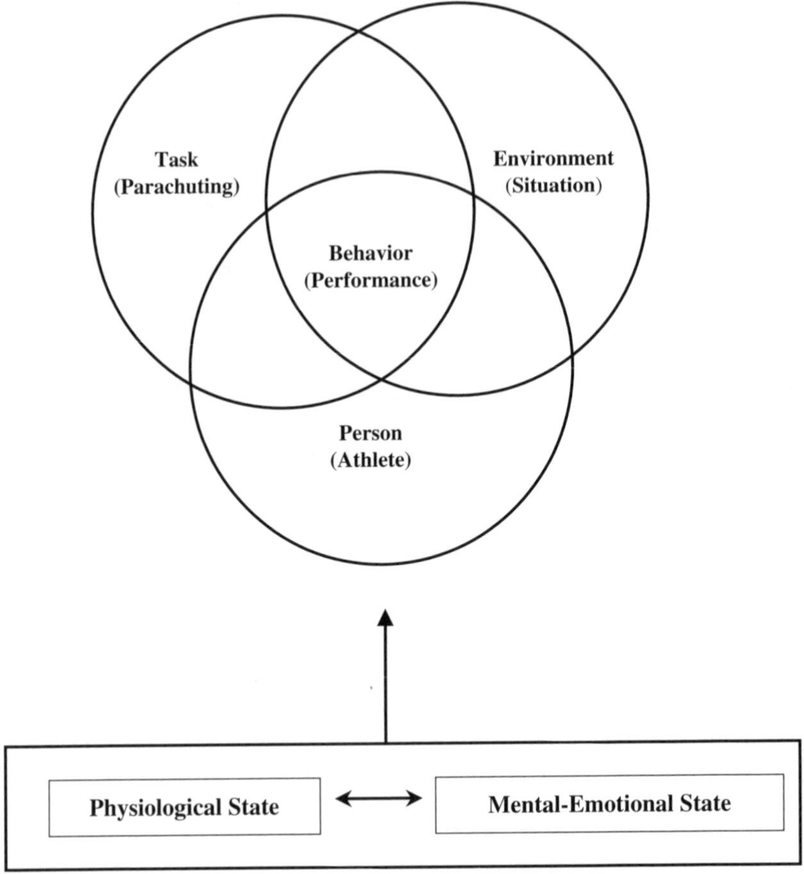

Figure 1.1 Performance (behavior) of athletes (parachutists) within a transactional system, taking into account the environment (situation) and "the psychophysiological principle", namely the interrelations between the physiological and the mental and emotional components of behavior

reality components as conceived and experienced by the behaving or performing individual.

Take, for example, a basketball player at the highest international level, who has to take a decisive shot in a highly critical situation during the final stage of an important close game (see Bar-Eli & Tractinsky, 2000). At face value, "a shot is a shot," but is it really so? Not necessarily: there is a considerable variance between the difficulty of shots not only on the "task" dimension (e.g., shots taken from different distances, with or without defending players, etc.), but also on the "environment" dimension: obviously, a shot taken in a low-criticality situation during another (i.e., not final) stage of a less important, not so close game would probably have meant "another shot" for the player! However, it is also reasonable to assume that more experienced players ("persons") who "have been in such movies" several times in their career, would not experience a substantial difference between these two "environments", which would probably in turn reflect on their perception of the "task" to be performed (e.g., in line with their level of expertise; see Summers, 1999).

In short: "tasks," "environments," and "persons" may, of course, "objectively" vary—for example, a basketball shot may be taken from different distances, under different weather conditions, and by players who differ in their shooting ability. Much more important, however, is the "subjective" facet of these action components, which in turn requires that they be conceptualized transactionally (Hackfort, 1994). From this perspective, the overlapping of the circles (see Figure 1.1) symbolizes the fact that "subjectively," separate existence of these components is actually meaningless (as the above-mentioned basketball example also demonstrates).

A further discussion is required in order to distinguish between the terms "behavior" and "performance." According to action theory (e.g., Frese & Zapf, 1994), performance should be conceived as a goal-directed behavior. A goal regulates human behavior, setting the acting person in a particular environment a standard to be achieved through task performance. Thus, "performance" is a more specific term than "behavior." In sport and exercise, such differences may be relevant, for example, in order to distinguish between elite athletes attempting to perform their best with a highly specific goal in mind (e.g., reaching the Olympic games), and nonelite (e.g., recreational) athletes, who are just "behaving," i.e., physically exercising without trying to realize any particular elite performance.

OBJECTIVE SUBJECTIVITY, SUBJECTIVE OBJECTIVITY: ON THE MEASUREMENT OF SPORT AND EXERCISE BEHAVIOR

Scientists investigating the psychophysiology of human behavior in sport and exercise settings can, in principle, always apply three possible levels of measurement: verbal (e.g., expressions of subjective experience, such as anxiety, inconvenience, or joy), motor (e.g., particular movements or facial expressions, observed behavior during games or practice), and physiological (e.g., increased pulse/breathing

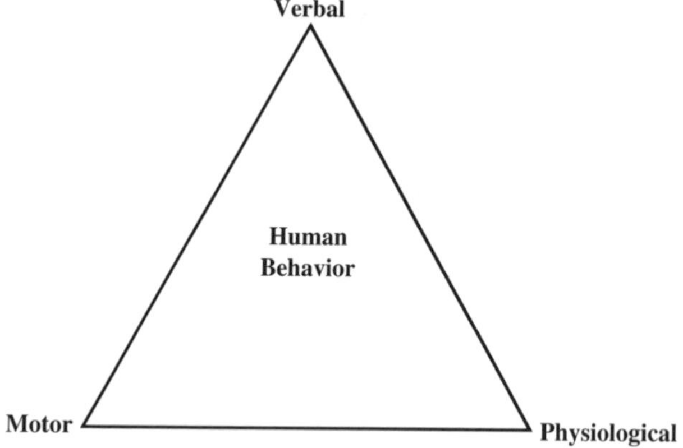

Figure 1.2 Measurement levels of human behavior

frequency or hormonal activity). These measurement levels are outlined schematically in Figure 1.2.

Almost two decades ago, Hatfield and Landers (1983) observed a (too) extensive reliance upon questionnaire-type data in the field of sport and exercise psychology. Hatfield and Landers (1983, p. 256) concluded their landmark article by stating that: "As the basis of psychophysiological theory and technology becomes more broadly developed, and law-like relations are discovered, the psychophysiological assessment of athletes promises to be useful in diagnosing performance problems and designing clinical interventions to overcome them."

Despite this quite optimistic view, Ostrow's (1996) monumental effort to catalogue sport and/or exercise measures over a 30-year period, which was followed by Duda's (1998) outstanding edited text on psychological measurement in sport and exercise settings, both reveal that in this sense no major changes have occurred. In other words, sport and exercise psychology still prefers to rely mainly on nonphysiological and/or nonobservational measures of behavior (see also Tenenbaum & Bar-Eli, 1995b). For example, Vealey and Garner-Holman's (1998) review of measurement issues in applied sport psychology claims that practitioners in this area typically use five types of methods to systematically assess athletes' thoughts, feelings, and behaviors: psychological inventories, survey questionnaires, interviews, behavioral observations, and psychophysiological measures. In the terms of Figure 1.2, the first three methods are "verbal" in nature, whereas the fourth and the fifth are "motor" and "physiological," respectively—which demonstrates an overwhelming dominance of "verbal" methods. Such methods are viewed as being "introspective" (i.e., "subjective") in nature, and the domain of sport and exercise psychology has often been criticized for relying too heavily upon the use of such techniques (e.g., Schutz, 1994).

It should be noted that since its earliest days (e.g., Thorndike, 1919; Thurstone, 1928), psychology has attempted to "objectivize" (i.e., quantify) this "subjectivity." This is quite evident at least with regard to psychological inventories and survey questionnaires, although much less so for the interview (Phares, 1992). At the same time, behavioral observations and physiological measures, which are seemingly more "objective," have often been the result of scientists' attempts to reduce natural complexity into relatively isolated units. Such units are "objectively manageable" but frequently meaningless without an accompanying "subjective" interpretation (Nitsch, 1997). Thus, the distinction between the terms "objective" and "subjective" is not quite clear-cut.

Bar-Eli (1997), for example, suggested an alternative approach to the regular practice of observing basketball players during competition, which was examined in two previous field studies. This author proposed the use of observables which are meaningful in terms of his crisis theory (see also Bar-Eli & Tractinsky, 2000). The observational tools applied in these studies were derived from the theory itself and were based on previous "verbal" questionnaire findings, which made these observations conceptually meaningful. Thus, following the use of an "objectivized subjectivity" (i.e., quantifiable questionnaires), a "subjectivized objectivity" (i.e., specifically developed observational grids) was applied to examine basketball players' performance in competition. As mentioned above, Falk and Bar-Eli (1995) applied a basically similar though somewhat less sophisticated research philosophy in their parachuting study, but with regard to the psychological ("verbal") and "physiological" corners of the triangle in Figure 1.2.

A MULTIDIMENSIONAL MODEL FOR BIOFEEDBACK RESEARCH AND APPLICATION IN SPORT AND EXERCISE

The term "biofeedback" refers to external psychophysiological feedback, physiological feedback, or augmented proprioception. The basic idea here is to provide individuals with information about what is going on inside their bodies, including their brains (Schwartz, 1979).

Psychophysiology in general and biofeedback in particular are overwhelmingly and typically conducted in laboratory settings (Andreassi, 2000). This state of affairs results in part from "built-in" limitations of biofeedback, such as cost and availability (Greenberg, 1983). Moreover, biofeedback devices are usually not designed for being used during real, daily stressful experiences, but rather for being used to train people to gain greater control of their physiological processes within the nonstressful laboratory setting (Crews, Lochbaum, & Karoly, 2001). It is therefore not surprising that in sport, biofeedback research has traditionally emphasized mainly closed skill sports, particularly target sports, which have offered the best avenue for biofeedback applications (Collins, 1995), at least in part because of their "laboratory-like" environments.

To gain more ecological validity within a transactional framework (see Tenenbaum & Bar-Eli, 1995a), sport and exercise psychology is in need of what Nitsch (1997, p. 22) called "a spiral sequence of field and laboratory studies." This statement applies also to sport- and exercise-related psychophysiological and/or biofeedback research. In addition, as both Tenenbaum and Bar-Eli (1995b) and Nitsch (1997) observed, the discipline of sport and exercise psychology has not yet satisfactorily integrated the computer into its repertoire of research and application. Computer simulations, for example, are viewed by these authors a promising way of introducing and manipulating realistic conditions in the sense of virtual realities, in order to study the dynamics of sport and exercise behavior under real-time and on-line conditions.

It can be concluded that in order to examine a sport/exercise-psychological theory, researchers are advised to conduct empirical investigations that integrate laboratory and field settings, together with computer simulations. As the above-cited extract from Hatfield and Landers (1983, p. 256) indicates, psychophysiological assessment of athletes should be useful primarily in terms of diagnosis and intervention. Figure 1.3

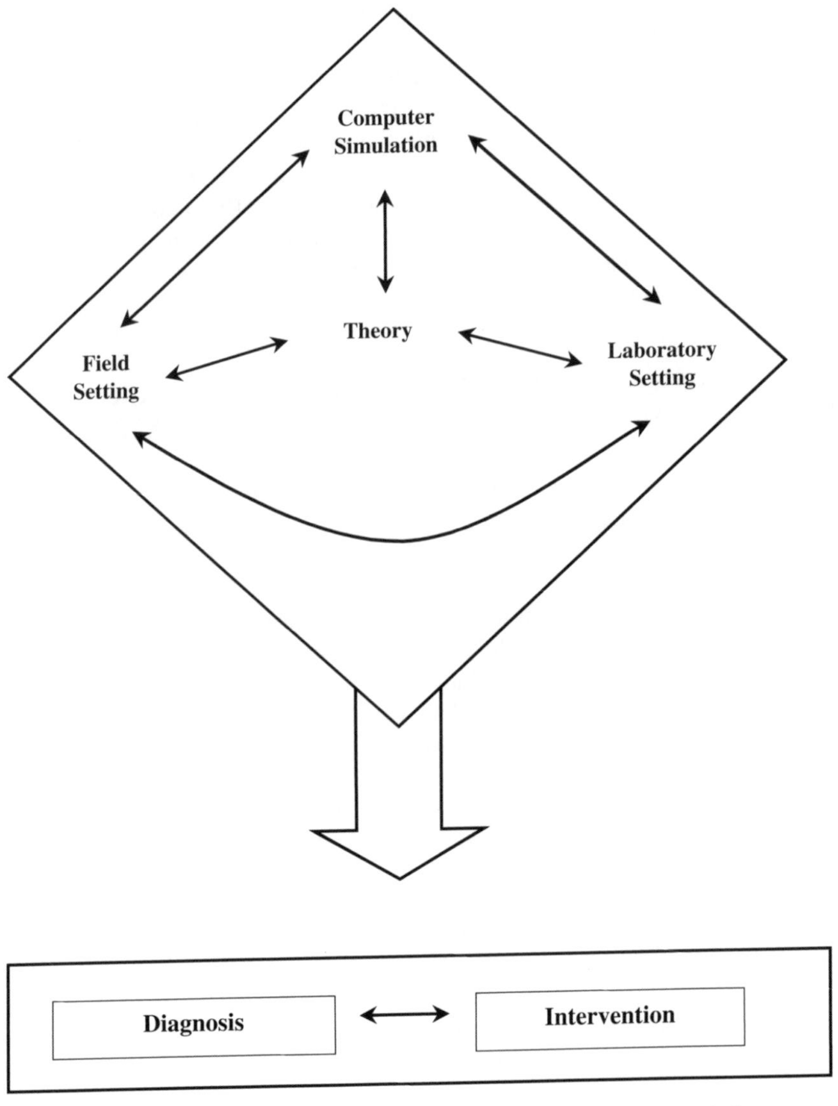

Figure 1.3 Multidimensional framework for applied biofeedback research in sport and exercise

presents a proposed multidimensional framework for applied biofeedback research in sport and exercise that integrates these ideas.

SOURCE AND NATURE OF SCIENTIFICALLY BASED ACTIONS: ON THE PROBLEMS BETWEEN PRACTITIONERS AND SPORT PSYCHOLOGISTS

The question of diagnosis and intervention requires further discussion from another point of view. More specifically, a practitioner's (e.g., athlete's) willingness to undergo a process of diagnosis and intervention often depends not only on the scientist's ability to provide the practitioner with appropriate psychophysiological (i.e., biofeedback-based) diagnostic and/or interventive tools, but also on the practitioner's readiness to accept them. As noted by Bar-Eli and Tenenbaum (1989), the collaboration between sport psychologists (and sport scientists in general) and practitioners may be disturbed as a result of different conceptions on the two sides as to the source and nature of diagnostic and/or interventive actions to be taken. More specifically, while the sport psychologist—acting as a consultant—should consider diagnostic and/or interventive actions scientifically (i.e., from an "internal" source) and treat them probabilistically (according to the regular state of scientifically based knowledge, which is probabilistic in nature), the practitioner (e.g., athlete or coach) often considers such subject matters from both "internal" and "external" sources (that is, also includes considerations which are not necessarily scientific, though important), and needs answers which are deterministic in nature, in order to enhance his or her performance.

Table 1.1 outlines the source and nature of scientifically based diagnostic and/or interventive actions conducted by sport psychologists and practitioners.

For example, when a sport psychologist interacts with a coach and proposes a biofeedback-based diagnosis–intervention program, such a proposal should in principle stem from an "internal" source, that is, relate primarily to actions studied and validated through theory and research conducted in this specific subject matter. However, the coach—the actual actor during competition and practice—often also takes into account matters such as his/her relationship with the athlete, the athlete's physical condition (e.g., injury, illness or fatigue), tactics and strategy, and the opponent's ability—i.e., considerations which are "external" with regard to the "pure" scientific subject matter. In other words, the coach's actions usually depend on "internal" and "external" sources of considerations.

Table 1.1 Source and nature of scientifically based actions conducted by sport psychologists and practitioners

	Actor	
Action	Sport psychologist	Practitioner
Source	Internal	Internal and external
Nature	Probabilistic	Deterministic

But moreover: scientists normally seek general conclusions. However, competitive sport usually cannot be sufficiently aided by general statements, but rather by relatively precise or definite instructions. Thus, when acting as a scientist, the sport psychologist should in fact supply recommendations which are probabilistic in nature (e.g., "This line of action may enhance the athlete's performance"), while the coach seeks more definite, deterministic instructions (e.g., "In order to enhance performance, you should imagine the rhythm of your steps when approaching the bar").

As a result, when a sport psychologist is asked to recommend a psychophysiologically based diagnosis–intervention plan of action for an athlete, he or she is often expected to supply a deterministic action plan, which would rely on both "internal" and "external" considerations. However, the best line of action the sport psychologist—acting as a scientific consultant—could recommend would be "internal" and probabilistic in nature. Because of this, it might disappoint the practitioner and/or be perceived by him/her as a failure on the part of the sport psychologist's failure, thus leading to possible disputes and misperceptions between the two.

ON THE CONCEPT OF SELF-REGULATION

Diagnosis and intervention are basically aimed at achieving self-regulation by the athletes. According to Schwartz (1979), self-regulation is an integral part of all mental diagnostic and/or interventive activities used to facilitate performance. An effectively self-regulated athlete would essentially function without the use of external controls, like on "automatic pilot," utilizing mainly self-perceived feedback. Athletes use "naive" or "intuitive" techniques to try and cope with fundamental psychoregulative problems or difficulties (Nitsch & Allmer, 1979). Systematic mental diagnosis and interventions (e.g., biofeedback-based programs such as the Wingate five-step approach presented in Chapter 4) are intended to teach the elite athlete and/or the nonelite exerciser alternative, scientific methods of self-regulation (Crews, 1993).

The concept of self-regulation is encompassed within "general systems theory" (e.g., Von Bertalanffy, 1968) that suggests that the behavior of a system (e.g., athlete, exerciser) is dependent on the dynamic, transactional contribution of its parts to the "Gestalt" as a whole. According to Schwartz (1979), the development of applied biofeedback is derived from cybernetics, a subset of general systems theory that addresses how a system becomes self-regulatory. Thus, the multidimensional approach presented in Figure 1.3 is closely related to this conceptual framework.

Practitioners and sport psychologists often collaborate to enhance athletes' self-regulation capabilities. However, such a continuous collaboration could also contribute to reducing the difference between their respective principal views concerning the source and nature of scientifically based diagnostic and/or interventive actions (see Figure 1.4). To further reduce this gap, person–task–environment specificities should be taken into account. For example, according to Bompa (1994), the key to successful athletic performance consists of organizing training programs from the *general* to the *specific*. In other words, the psychophysiological aspect of an athlete's preparation should not only be integrated into the training program in conjunction with its other parameters (i.e., the physical, technical, and tactical elements), but should also reflect this very basic principle of proceeding from the general to the specific.

The Wingate five-step approach to mental training in sport (incorporating biofeedback), outlined in more detail elsewhere in this volume, was developed in line with this important principle. Accordingly, this program, which is aimed at the enhancement of athletes' self-regulation capabilities, is highly flexible in its ability to adapt to match specific needs of individual athletes fulfilling particular discipline-specific tasks within given environments (Blumenstein & Bar-Eli, 2001). In this way, the program also provides more deterministic answers to the practitioners, taking into account more of their "external" considerations—thereby reducing some of the gap between practitioners and sport psychologists (see Figure 1.4). From a more general perspective, this approach reflects the basic action-theoretical idea that real, everyday self-regulated motor behavior should be conceived as "behavior in situation" (Nitsch, 1994)—an idea which has been deeply rooted in general psychology for many years (e.g., Cronbach, 1957; Pervin, 1977).

It should be noted that, due to their dynamic nature (see Von Bertalanffy, 1968), in such self-regulated systems diagnosis and intervention often act together. For instance, Blumenstein, Bar-Eli, and Tenenbaum (1997) proposed that the self-regulation test (SRT) of arousal be used to examine athletes' self-regulation level before and during the application of their mental training program ("five-step approach"). Thus, diagnosis and intervention are used here as integral parts of one entire dynamic process specifically designed to enhance self-regulation capability and facilitate performance.

SUMMARY, CONCLUSIONS, AND FUTURE DIRECTIONS

To formally summarize and define the content of variables discussed thus far, a mapping sentence will be used. A mapping sentence (a concept formulated in the 1950s by Guttman; see Levy, 1994) is comprised of facets, which are sets of attributes that in some sense belong together, and that represent underlying conceptual and semantic components of a content universe. If components of a content universe are described by *n* facets, then any variable from that universe would be denoted by one element for each of these *n* facets. This combination of elements (called a "structuple") summarizes the conceptual components of the variable (Dancer, 1990).

The summarizing mapping sentence used to synthesize the factors and variables reviewed here is the following:

> Biofeedback applications, {generally/specifically} oriented towards the self-regulation of {sport/exercise} {behavior/performance}, are based on {self-/inter-trans-}actional theories concerning the relations between {persons/environments/tasks} and {physiological/mental-emotional} states, measured {objectively/subjectively} on the {verbal/motor/physiological} level in {laboratory

settings/field settings/computer simulations}, for the purpose of taking {diagnostic/interventive} actions, which are of a {probabilistic/deterministic} nature and stem from an {internal/external} source.

This mapping sentence encompasses the entire frame of content discussed in this chapter, and at the same time provides a conceptual framework for future research and application. For example, one could produce profiles that represent possible combinations among the various variables. Such profiles can be useful for a better understanding of scientifically based psychophysiological/biofeedback research and application in sport and exercise.

This chapter can be considered a significant step toward a formation of a psychophysiological "meta-theory" on biofeedback applications in sport and exercise. Concepts derived from various theories of self-regulation (e.g., Kuhl, 1992) could be incorporated into such a "meta-theory", which could then provide a transactional framework to help explain the contributions of such "subtheories." Complexity in theory, research, and practice is inevitable here, considering the complexity of the constructs and relations involved. Therefore, co-operation among researchers and practitioners in this area should be encouraged, so that these issues may be fruitfully addressed in the years to come, in line with the current and future agendas of sport/exercise science in general and sport/exercise psychology in particular.

REFERENCES

Andreassi, J. L. (2000). *Psychophysiology: Human behavior and physiological response* (4th ed.). Hillsdale, NJ: Erlbaum.

Bandura, A. (1997). *Self-efficacy: The exercise of control.* New York: Freeman.

Bar-Eli, M. (1997). Psychological performance crisis in competition, 1984–1996: A review. *European Yearbook of Sport Psychology*, **1**, 73–112.

Bar-Eli, M., & Tenenbaum, G. (1989). Coach-psychologist relations in competitive sport. In A. D. LeUnes, J. S. Picou, & W. K. Simpson (eds.), *Applied research in coaching and athletics, annual* (pp. 150–156). Boston, MA: American Press.

Bar-Eli, M., & Tractinsky, N. (2000). Criticality of game situations and decision making in basketball: An application of performance crisis perspective. *Psychology of Sport and Exercise*, **1**, 27–39.

Blanchard, E. B., & Epstein, L. H. (1978). *A biofeedback primer.* Reading, MA: Addison-Wesley.

Blumenstein, B., Bar-Eli, M., & Tenenbaum, G. (1997). A five-step approach to mental training incorporating biofeedback. *The Sport Psychologist*, **11**, 440–453.

Blumenstein, B., & Bar-Eli, M. (2001). A five-step approach for biofeedback training in sport. *Sportwissenschaft*. (31)4, 412–424.

Bompa, T. (1994). *Theory and methodology of training: The key to athletic performance* (3rd ed.). Dubuque, IA: Kendall/Hunt.

Collins, D. (1995). Psychophysiology and sport performance. In S. J. H. Biddle (ed.), *European perspectives on exercise and sport psychology* (pp. 154–178). Champaign, IL: Human Kinetics.

Crews, D. J. (1993). Self-regulation strategies in sport and exercise. In R. N. Singer, M. Murphey, & L. K. Tennant (eds.), *Handbook of research on sport psychology* (pp. 557–568). New York: Macmillan.

Crews, D., Lochbaum, M., & Karoly, P. (2001). Self-regulation: Concepts, methods and strategies in sport and exercise. In R. Singer, H. Hausenblas, & C. Janelle (eds.), *Handbook of sport psychology* (pp. 566–581) (2nd ed.). New York: J. Willey & Sons.

Cronbach, L. J. (1957). The two disciplines of scientific psychology. *American Psychologist*, **12**, 671–684.

Dancer, L. S. (1990). Introduction to facet theory and its application. *Applied Psychology*, **39**, 365–377.

Dewey, J., & Bentley, A. F. (1949). *Knowing and the known*. Boston, MA: Beacon.

Duda, J. L. (ed.). (1998). *Advances in sport and exercise psychology measurement*. Morgantown, WV: Fitness Information Technology.

Ekehammar, B. (1974). Interactionism in personality from a historical perspective. *Psychological Bulletin*, **81**, 1026–1048.

Falk, B., & Bar-Eli, M. (1995). The psycho-physiological response to parachuting among novice and experienced parachutists. *Aviation, Space and Environmental Medicine*, **66**, 114–117.

Frese, M., & Zapf, D. (1994). Action as the core of work psychology: A German approach. In H. C. Triandis, M. D. Dunnette, & L. M. Haugh (Eds.), *Handbook of industrial and organizational psychology* (vol. 4, pp. 271–340). Palo Alto, CA: Consulting Psychologist.

Green, E., Green, A. M., & Walters, E. D. (1970). Voluntary control of internal states: Psychological and physiological. *Journal of Transpersonal Psychology*, **2**, 1–26.

Greenberg, J. S. (1983). *Comprehensive stress management*. Dubuque, IA: Wm. C. Brown.

Hackfort, D. (1994). Health and wellness: A sport psychology perspective. In S. Serpa, J. Alves, & U. Pataco (eds.), *International perspectives on sport and exercise psychology* (pp. 165–183). Morgantown, WV: Fitness Information Technology.

Hatfield, B. D., & Landers, D. M. (1983). Psychophysiology—A new direction for sport psychology. *Journal of Sport Psychology*, **5**, 243–259.

Kuhl, J. (1992). A theory of self-regulation: Action versus state orientation, self-discrimination and some applications. *Applied Psychology*, **41**, 97–129.

Levy, S. (ed.). (1994). *Louis Guttman on theory and methodology: Selected writings*. Aldershot: Dartmouth Benchmark.

Moss, D. (ed.). (1994). *Twenty-fifth anniversary yearbook*. Wheat Ridge, CO: Association for Applied Psychophysiology and Biofeedback.

Moss, D. (ed.). (1998). *Humanistic and transpersonal psychology: An historical and biographical sourcebook*. Westport, CT: Greenwood.

Neiss, R. (1988). Reconceptualizing arousal: Psychological states in motor performance. *Psychological Bulletin*, **103**, 345–366.

Nitsch, J. R. (1994). The organization of motor behavior. An action-theoretical perspective. In J. R. Nitsch & R. Seiler (eds.), *Movement and sport. Psychological foundations and effects: vol. 2. Motor control and motor learning* (Proceedings of the VIIIth European Congress of Sport Psychology 1991 in Cologne, pp. 3–21). Sankt Augustin, Germany: Academia.

Nitsch, J. R. (1997). Empirical research in sport psychology: A critical review of the laboratory–field controversy. *European Yearbook of Sport Psychology*, **1**, 1–28.

Nitsch, J. R., & Allmer, H. (1979). Naive psychoregulative Techniken der Selbstbeeinflussung im Sport [Naive psychoregulative techniques of self-influence in sport]. *Sportwissenschaft*, **9**, 143–163.

Nitsch, J. R., & Munzert, J. (1997). Handlungstheoretische Aspekte des Techniktrainings: Ansätze zu einem integrativen Modell [Action theoretical aspects of coaching techniques: Towards an integrative model]. In J. R. Nitsch, A. Neumaier, H. de Marées, & J. Mester (eds.), *Techniktraining: Beiträge zu einem interdisziplinären Ansatz [Techniques coaching: Contributions to an interdisciplinary approach]* (pp. 109–172). Schorndorf: Hofmann.

Ostrow, A. C. (1996). *Directory of psychological tests in the sport and exercise sciences* (2nd ed.). Morgantown, WV: Fitness Information Technology.

Pervin, L. A. (1977). The representative design of person-situation research. In D. Magnusson & N. S. Endler (eds.), *Personality at the crossroads: Current issues in interactional psychology* (pp. 371–384). Hillsdale, NJ: Erlbaum.

Pervin, L. A. (1985). Personality: Current controversies, issues, and directions. *Annual Review of Psychology*, **36**, 83–114.

Phares, E. J. (1992). *Clinical psychology: Concepts, methods, and profession* (4th ed.). Belmont, CA: Brooks/Cole.

Raglin, J. S. (1992). Anxiety and sport performance. In J. O. Holoszy (ed.), *Exercise and sport sciences review* (vol. 20, pp. 243–274). Baltimore: Williams & Wilkins.

Schutz, R. W. (1994). Methodological issues and measurement problems in sport psychology. In S. Serpa, J. Alves, & U. Pataco (eds.), *International perspectives on sport and exercise psychology* (pp. 35–56). Morgantown, WV: Fitness Information Technnology.

Schwartz, G. E. (1979). Disregulation and systems theory: A biobehavioral framework for biofeedback and behavioral medicine. In N. Birbaumer & H. D. Kimmel (eds.), *Biofeedback and self-regulation* (pp. 19–48). New York: Erlbaum.

Summers, J. J. (1999). Skill acquisition: Current perspectives and future directions. In R. Lidor & M. Bar-Eli (eds.), *Sport psychology: Linking theory and practice* (pp. 83–107). Morgantown, WV: Fitness Information Technology.

Tenenbaum, G., & Bar-Eli, M. (1995a). Personality and intellectual capabilities in sport psychology. In D. H. Saklofske & M. Zeidner (eds.), *International handbook of personality and intelligence* (pp. 687–710). New York: Plenum.

Tenenbaum, G., & Bar-Eli, M. (1995b). Contemporary issues in exercise and sport psychology research. In S. J. H. Biddle (ed.), *European perspectives on exercise and sport psychology* (pp. 292–323). Champaign, IL: Human Kinetics.

Thorndike, E. L. (1919). *An introduction to the theory of mental and social measurements.* New York: Teachers' College, Columbia.

Thurstone, L. L. (1928). The measurement of opinion. *Journal of Abnormal and Social Psychology*, **22**, 415–430.

Vealey, R. S., & Garner-Holman, M. (1998). Applied sport psychology: Measurement issues. In J. L. Duda (ed.), *Advances in sport and exercise psychology measurement* (pp. 431–446). Morgantown, WV: Fitness Information Technology.

Von Bertalanffy, L. (1968). *General systems theory*. New York: Braziller.

Zaichkowsky, L. D. (1983). The use of biofeedback for self-regulation of performance states. In L.-E. Unestahl (ed.), *The mental aspects of gymnastics* (pp. 95–105). Örebro, Sweden: Veje.

CHAPTER 2

Psychophysiology and Athletic Performance

Dave Collins

INTRODUCTION

Biofeedback is an increasingly common and extremely useful tool for applied sport psychologists and a text dedicated to its application is well overdue. Two problems limit its optimum usage however. Firstly, the hardware-intensive nature of biofeedback has led many "technophobic" colleagues to dive for cover and avoid its use. Indeed, some have even exhibited a backlash response, questioning the efficacy of biofeedback by reference to poor applications or misapplications of the technique. Hopefully this text, coupled with more comprehensive professional preparation programmes, will lead to a greater acceptance and employment of what is, unquestionably, a useful adjunct to almost all approaches in applied sport psychology as well as a significant intervention in itself.

The second and related problem is harder to address, however. Obviously, biofeedback draws on the significant research area of psychophysiology as the basis for its use. A fairly comprehensive knowledge of this topic, and even more crucially a reasonable understanding of its strengths and weaknesses, is an important prerequisite of effective biofeedback employment. In other words, professional preparation programmes need to develop a genuine feel for psychophysiology if practitioners are to design, develop, and apply new and innovative approaches rather than just use the recipes included with the equipment manual.

The point is exemplified by a parallel development, namely the increasing employment of user-friendly statistical packages. In the "good old days", complexity of programming and interpretation limited use of the more sophisticated statistical techniques to those possessing at least a semblance of understanding of what was going on in the calculation process. Latterly, however, nice clear instructions have enabled a proliferation of multivariate and equation modelling approaches that are easily accessible to researchers, informed and uninformed alike, at the click of a mouse button.

Brain and Body in Sport and Exercise: Biofeedback Applications in Performance Enhancement.
Edited by Boris Blumenstein, Michael Bar-Eli, and Gershon Tenenbaum.

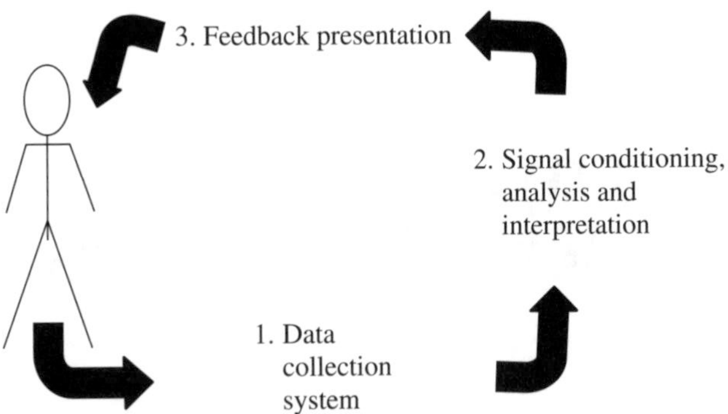

Figure 2.1 The three essential stages of a biofeedback system

Unfortunately, therefore, many investigations display the use of extremely complex statistics that either fail to meet the necessary underlying assumptions for their use or are completely misapplied. In similar fashion, well-designed and easy-to-use biofeedback units, together with other comparatively simple psychophysiological equipment, have resulted in a welcome increase in the use of such techniques *but* not always in the most efficacious fashion. So, if you wish to make best use of biofeedback, make sure that you have a good idea of the underlying psychophysiological mechanisms and technical considerations before you start.

These concerns have driven the design of this chapter. My aim is to offer a comprehensive overview of psychophysiology concepts pertinent to biofeedback, together with the basic structures and technical methodologies used. I hope that experienced colleagues will find the overview useful, whilst those wishing to make a start in biofeedback will feel energised to get stuck in to the psychophysiology textbooks.

A good starting point is to consider the three central elements of any biofeedback system: (1) data collection, (2) analysis and interpretation, and (3) feedback presentation (Figure 2.1). The first and second stages are built on psychophysiology, and consideration of this discipline forms the bulk of this chapter. Stage three receives a much briefer review since it is considered in more detail elsewhere in the book.

One other essential item is necessary before you start your "psychophysiology primer". Figure 2.2 presents an imaginary waveform but serves to introduce or summarise some of the key terms which are essential for subsequent discussion. Consider these factors, and how they may interact, as you read the subsequent sections.

METHODS IN PSYCHOPHYSIOLOGY

Psychophysiology is an underused approach in sport psychology. This is unfortunate, since it offers an almost unique insight into mental processes and, through approaches such as biofeedback, can form the basis of an extremely effective intervention. Defined as "the scientific study of cognitive, emotional and behavioural phenomena as related

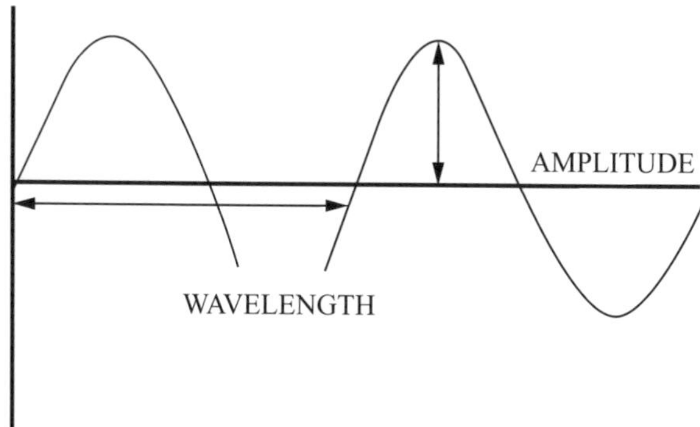

Figure 2.2 Waveform terminology

to and revealed through physiological principles and events" (Cacioppo & Tassinary, 1990, p. ix), the approach can provide an objective and relatively non-invasive method of examining the complex processes involved in sport performance as they take place. The attraction of such an ecologically valid technique over the more usual self-report approach is obvious, and several reviews (e.g. Smith & Collins, 1991) identify sport psychophysiology as an important and current research thrust.

There are problems, however. First of all, studies in "mainstream" psychophysiology, whilst they address topics relevant to sport, can seem too esoteric and scholarly for those more interested in application. Even worse, but also apparent, are the over-simplified generalisations which are often made from such studies. In fact, many of these pitfalls can be avoided if research consumers gain a basic understanding of the methods and constructs themselves, enabling an informed sorting of "wheat from the chaff" and an ability to detect the more over-the-top claims made by some equipment providers.

The second concern relates to the interpretation of the physiological signals. The measurement of "harder data"—and if psychophysiology does anything well, it certainly provides you with loads of numbers—is extremely appealing but can also prove seductive. In short, a genuine trap of *over*-interpretation exists for the uninformed or unwary novice. Sometimes, investigators fall into the trap of searching for correlation between measures and self-reported conditions or outcome behaviours, rather than considering the chain of causation which links them (cf. Donchin & Coles, 1988; Zani & Rossi, 1991a). Correct application of psychophysiology requires that the physiological events recorded are interpreted by reference to their underlying mechanisms, and not just identified as a convenient concomitant of an assumed mental set or behaviour. Sadly, this has not always been remembered in sport-related studies.

For these and other reasons, a knowledge of "how and why it works" is essential, spanning both the acquisition and the underlying causes of psychophysiological data. The remaining sections offer a primer on these key considerations.

Data Collection

Figure 2.1 includes the crucial factors which underpin psychophysiology, namely data collection, signal conditioning and interpretation. Data collection in psychophysiology requires that the electrophysiological signal is "pure": basically uncontaminated and artefact-free. First let's consider the contamination. When pairs of electrodes are attached to a body, a wide variety of signals are received, only one of which is generally of interest. Thus, for example, electrodes attached to the scalp to detect brain activity (the electroencephalogram, or EEG) will be substantially inconvenienced by signals which result from all the other things going on in the body. For example, the regular heartbeat signal is so strong that it can pervade all parts of the body. To counter this, psychophysiology amplifiers are designed with high "common mode rejection", a characteristic that means that signals which appear at both electrode sites are dismissed from consideration. Having lost the unrequired heartbeat, differences between the two electrodes are then considered. This idea of using a "reference" electrode is common to many types of psychophysiological measurement. An additional, "ground" electrode is also useful for this purpose whilst also enabling the data collection system to dismiss any other signals that are affecting the whole body such as radio transmissions. Even so, contaminating signals can still be a problem, particularly when they are much stronger than the signal of interest. This is a common problem in EEG, where muscle activity associated with eye blinks, jaw clenching, etc., is so much larger than the comparatively weak electrical signals of the brain through the skull that it completely overpowers the signals of interest.

The other major challenge relates to the artefactual signals generated by relative movements between the skin and the electrode. Electrical signals from the skin are normally passed to the electrode (and thence to the amplification and signal conditioning system) by an electrolytic paste. Since all three elements of this chain have different electrical potentials, artefactual signals are generated when one of them moves relative to the others, through a mechanism that is somewhat similar to a mini-generator. Once again, this is a particular problem for low-power signals like EEG, but in all cases firm attachment of the electrode represents an essential first step towards minimising the problem. Preparation of the skin surface to minimise electrical resistance is also crucial; indeed, any reputable study in this area will always report the steps taken and levels of resistance obtained (in ohms) as a result. Essentially, this relates to abrasion of the surface for the removal of grease, grime and dead skin cells, enabling a link to be made directly with the inner sections of the epidermis. In anticipation of your first "prep", or just in case you are ever a subject for an overly enthusiastic investigator, please note that it is easy to over-abrade the surface; indeed, blood flow, quite apart from the health danger which it may represent, also increases resistance and renders the site useless. Try to explain this in between your screams!

A basic grounding in electrical theory should also highlight the possible problem that can occur between pairs of electrodes. If one electrode–paste–skin combination has very different resistances to the other, this will offer another source of artefactual signal. Accordingly, it is important that resistance levels are not only low but also homogeneous across the sites used.

The choice of different electrode and electrolytic paste materials is another key consideration and, for a variety of technical reasons, silver–silver chloride electrodes are the most common materials used at present. The age and condition of the materials, extending even to staying within the sell-by date of the paste itself, are also important. The selection and upkeep of electrodes, choosing the optimum electrolyte for the job, and quick and effective fitting of an electrode montage all represent tasks which require a fair amount of technical expertise. In our own laboratory, "practice makes perfect" is the watchword, and all new researchers complete an apprenticeship after receiving training in these black arts.

Signal Conditioning

Assuming that the signals emanating from the skin–electrolyte–electrode combination are genuine and artefact-free, there are still a number of potential pitfalls that can obscure the quality of the final data. The most logical procedure is to consider these in the order that they appear.

First of all, problems can occur because of the comparatively weak signals that are common to psychophysiology, especially in comparison to the size of the electrical signals, including the mains supply, that are present elsewhere in the recording system. These other signals are referred to as "noise" and, just as with your music system at home, a good signal-to-noise ratio is an essential characteristic for the amplifiers used. As the previous sections showed, however, there are lots of other noise sources and, accordingly, amplification of the signal at the earliest possible opportunity can serve to inoculate the signal against contamination. Thus, EEG signals are often amplified very close to the collection site by a unit known as a head-box. The strengthened signals, with accordingly better signal-to-noise ratios, are then passed to another amplification system. In other cases—examination of muscular activity (electromyography or EMG), for example—electrodes are commonly wired so that signals are passed directly (less than 3 cm of wire connection) to a small pre-amplifier before direct or radio transmission to the main amplification systems. As a result of this approach, the signal is more robust against contamination, although considerable steps are still taken to keep the noise as low as possible. Accordingly, shielded wires are always used, with lengths kept to a minimum. The data collection environment can also be usefully considered, with background electrical signals (mains boxes, high-tension cables etc.) re-routed away from the lab. Even certain sorts of lighting can cause a problem here, so it is worth taking your time with the design of psychophysiology labs. Finally, static-free floor surfaces are a must. We enjoyed hours of endless fun and lots of abuse from the architects of our new labs when we pulled up all the newly laid carpet tiles to prevent static build-up on subjects and investigators!

Having got the signals to the amplifier, further steps are necessary to ensure that the resulting data are an accurate representation of the truth. Filtering of the signal

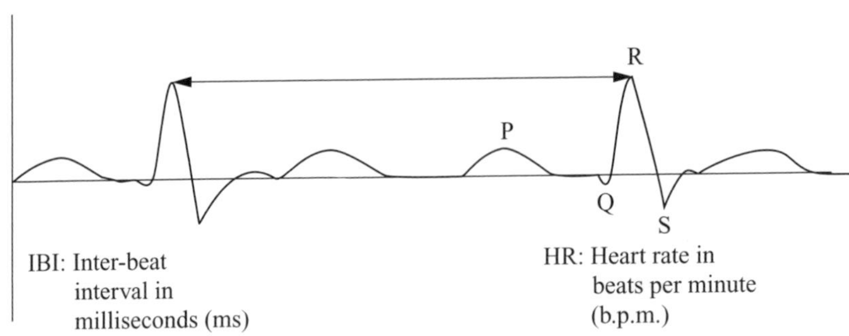

Figure 2.3 The cardiac cycle waveform and two possible derivatives: inter-beat interval and heart rate

is essential in order to remove both artefacts and other psychophysiological signals which may not be of interest. Once again, informed and considered decisions are necessary to get this right. Some things are easy; for example, systems almost always include a "notch" filter that removes any contamination at the frequency of the local mains signal [50 cycles per second or hertz (Hz) in the UK, 60 Hz in many other places]. There is likely to be no interest in this signal under any circumstances! Other decisions can be more complex, however, and affect both the lower and higher limits of the signals considered: should signals less than 0.2 Hz but greater than 40 Hz be dismissed in EEG investigations, for example? Complete consideration of these subtle issues is beyond the scope of this chapter but, as a simple quality control measure, make sure that papers and technical reports include both the conditioning applied and the rationale for the more complicated decisions taken—usually through reference to other published work. Amplification is another related issue and, once again, most investigations will use standardised or previously employed approaches.

Once the signal is available, the investigator needs to decide exactly which bit is of interest. In most cases, psychophysiological indices emerge as an analogue waveform generated by the activity. The classic PQRS wave of cardiac activity shown in Figure 2.3 is an example of this. In many cases, however, numerical data that provide a more quantitative viewpoint on some aspect of the activity are used instead. Thus, the cardiac waveform can be "converted" to the heart rate by counting the number of complete cycles occuring in a minute (HR in beats per minute, b.p.m.), a process usually completed automatically by detection of the large "R" spikes. If we are interested in more phasic changes, however, the times for each cycle can be calculated as the inter-beat interval (IBI in milliseconds). In either case—and many other digital representations are possible—the numbers represent a more convenient but less accurate approximation of the complete picture than the one offered by the analogue waveform.

Ever more complex digital representations are possible and, in fact, the application of digital amplification techniques makes consideration of these issues important even when the analogue waveform is used. As before, some aspect of the analogue data is summarised by these indices. Such numbers can represent amplitude or power (the "size" of the signal), the frequency or rate, change from baseline (typically labelled "delta", Δ), etc., and these indices may be expressed in standard (e.g. beats per minute, milliseconds, microvolts) or arbitary units. This process of digitisation (changing the analogue waveform signal into numbers suitable for display or manipulation) requires an analogue (waveform)-to-digital (number) or A-to-D converter to take a series of "pictures" or samples of the waveform over a finite time period. Faster sampling (usually expressed in number of samples per second or hertz—but don't confuse this number with filtering information) is usually better because it generates a more accurate picture. The idea is somewhat akin to that of increasing sample size in a standard research paradigm. If the sampling rate is too slow (insufficient subjects), artefactual signals (an inaccurate and often extreme picture) can be generated which can almost nullify conclusions drawn from the resulting data. Any reputable study should provide information about these factors (the signal conditioning performed), so beware of those which gloss over this topic! Certainly, as a simple rule, sampling rates should be at least four times the highest frequency of interest. Thus collection of EEG signals up to 40 Hz requires sampling rates of at least 256 Hz, since, for technical and mathematical reasons, options increase binomially thus 32–64–128–256–512, etc.

In summary, the main take-home message is that effective psychophysiology, and consequently effective biofeedback, is built on a series of sound technical decisions. This is an important factor, and critical consideration of these elements should form a central part of the reading strategy for the critical research consumer in this area.

One final word is necessary about the increasing use of "intelligent" interfaces such as the Keithley, CED or Biodata systems (Keithley Instruments, Inc., Cleveland, Ohio; Cambridge Electronic Design, Cambridge, UK; Biodata Ltd., Manchester, UK). These computer-based units can offer programmable options in A-to-D conversion, amplification and signal conditioning, whilst also "driving" the experiment through fine timing of stimulus administration, response timing and script-based, programmable analysis. Simply put, they are increasingly an essential for the self-respecting psychophysiology lab. Only one drawback, however. As with all the other automations identified, care must be taken to ensure that what is programmed is what is wanted. As with any computerised system, the GIGO rule (garbage in, garbage out) means that extra care is necessary since so much is going on out of the sight of the investigator. Manual checks and inspections of sample data will go a long way towards protecting the unsuspecting researcher against rather odd, gremlin-induced results.

Interpretation

There are a wide variety of indices that can be examined in sport psychophysiology, and almost all of these can be effectively employed in biofeedback settings (see Chapter 4 for a complete treatment of these). However, for effective usage, the interpretation and "causation not correlation" issues highlighted earlier in the chapter have to be addressed. An example will help to make this clear.

Heart rate is a commonly used index in sport psychophysiology, and several investigations have shown a general tendency for HR deceleration to be a sign of effective preparation. Thus, HR deceleration has been shown to be typical of better performers and better performance in archery (Wang & Landers, 1987) and golf putting (Boutcher & Zinsser, 1990), although such an effect was notably absent in a later archery study (Salazar, Landers, Petruzello, Han, Crews, & Kubitz, 1990). In fact, these inconsistencies may be due to the metabolically appropriate nature of the change, which relates in turn to the demands of the sport. Interpretation of psychophysiological signals is often based on the principle that the changes observed are metabolically inappropriate, and thus indicative of central cognitive or meta-cognitive events rather than simple physical preparation or exertion. Getting ready for a major muscular effort, a weight lift for example, will require considerable physical preparation, and it is likely that the general "geeing up" of the system that takes place will mask or confound more subtle changes, such as those due to an increased mental focus. In archery, drawing and holding the bow at full draw will elevate the HR, and this may mask far smaller HR changes which are associated with mental activity. Point no. 1, then, is to ensure that the changes you see (and promote through biofeedback) are genuine concomitants of mental state, not just simple changes associated with getting ready for the physical demands of the task.

These inconsistencies notwithstanding, HR deceleration appears to be a robust effect and it should be noted that in the golf study, where no metabolic, task-related demands were present to elevate the HR (golf putting is pretty easy—physically, at any rate), there was a positive correlation between the magnitude of deceleration prior to the putt and eventual levels of performance—a finding with important implications for biofeedback-based interventions. But now consider what may occur if a biofeedback intervention "merely requires" a decrease in HR as part of the preparation for the putt. The simplest way to lower HR is to hold your breath, at least for a short period! The golfer-athlete receiving the intervention, and indeed the researcher examining the effect, have to be aware that the HR change observed in the original investigation was cognitively mediated, and try to accomplish the biofeedback-promoted changes through such means. Thus, point no. 2 is that the nature of the physiological effect must be understood through triangulation with performance data *and* post-hoc self-report on what the athlete was trying to achieve mentally. Only then will provision of information about what the system is doing (a key facet of biofeedback itself) result in appropriate changes.

Finally, then, consider what is happening mentally, and what the athlete should try to achieve. Exactly why the deceleration effect occurs is still a matter of debate. The cardiac coupling hypothesis (Obrist, Howard, Lawler, Galosy, Meyers, & Gaelein, 1974) suggests that HR deceleration is a concomitant to motor quietening associated with a more internal focus. In contrast, however, the intake-rejection hypothesis (Lacey & Lacey, 1970) suggests an opposite mechanism. Under this hypothesis, tasks requiring outwardly directed attention (intake tasks) are associated with decreased activation, whilst rejection tasks (an inward orientation) result in general increases in arousal measures. So should the golfer promote external stimulus detection/intake, increase vigilance to ensure detection of pertinent information about the green, for example, or focus internally (rejection) on the execution of a smooth, well-learned technique? This is where consideration of other variables and ideas will direct one towards the latter, and encourage the golfer through other media, such as biofeedback on his putting mechanics, to focus on execution of an effective internalised plan. In other words, is it what is thought that is important, rather than the fact that focus is increased? If so—and this certainly makes intuitive sense for many sporting situations—then "simply" considering and/or encouraging HR change could have a limited or even a detrimental effect. Hence point no. 3: make sure that you focus on the causative factor for the performance, not merely one that is associated with it.

These caveats will underpin much of the work apparent in this book; in fact, other work from our lab related to examination of these very issues will be presented in Chapter 4. In the meantime, however, I will consider the range of indices that have been used in psychophysiology, together with some brief details and considerations for their use.

CONSTRUCTS, CONCEPTS AND APPLICATIONS IN PSYCHOPHYSIOLOGY

It is hard to know how best to consider the range of measures available, since several can be used for different purposes. For clarity, therefore, this brief overview focuses on the constructs through consideration of four of the practical situations in which they can be deployed, with brief descriptions of the modalities offered as and when they first appear. To aid clarity, key terms are *italicised*. The interested reader is referred to Cacioppo and Tassinary (1990) for a detailed review of the technical and theoretical considerations pertaining to each index.

Arousal–Excitation States

Given the volume of research attention which the topic of arousal–excitation states has received, it is no surprise to find that a number of psychophysiological techniques have been applied to its examination. The use of physiological indices is intuitive in this setting, and almost every technique has been used. Accordingly, higher arousal has been associated with a variety of metabolic measures such as increased *HR*, increased *blood pressure* (BP), *respiration rate* (RR), and decreased *respiration depth* assayed through tidal volume (the amount of air shifted in and out with each breath). As an example of this approach, consider the classic study of expert and novice free-fall parachutists by Fenz and Epstein in 1967. In this investigation, experts were shown to be more relaxed than novices and, more crucially, to demonstrate a differential time path for arousal, through consideration of HR data collected prior to, in direct preparation for, during and after jumping. In simple terms, average HR was lower for the experts and peaked as they arrived at the airfield, as contrasted to novices who exhibited "rather large" HR readings just before they left the aircraft.

As described earlier in the chapter, HR is usually derived from the full cardiac waveform, which can itself be collected through simple pulse-meter-style watches or more sophisticated, medically orientated set-ups. In the case of the former, sampling and storage rates can become an issue, especially since several of the commercially available units will average HR over a number of seconds, storing a series of mean values in order to achieve longer collection intervals. RR and other respiratory measures can be collected through the use of comparatively simple equipment consisting of transducers, amplifiers and A-to-D converters; at this basic level, collection or interpretation is rarely problematic. BP is also a useful measure, although the need for a pressure cuff, which must inflate and deflate to detect BP, does represent a limitation to the use of this measure in some settings.

Central measures of *EEG* related to arousal are based on the quantity or "power" of alpha rhythm, the 8- to 13-Hz signal emanating from the occipital (visual) cortex, a signal which has traditionally been related to a state of quiescence or relaxation across the brain. *Electromyography* or EMG has also been used in this context, with increased arousal associated with greater muscle activity or resting tone in various muscle groups such as the corrugator (frowning) muscles on the forehead, a measure commonly referred to as frontalis (forehead) EMG. More detailed consideration of these two measures is presented in subsequent sections.

Finally, the impact of general metabolic increase has been considered through peripheral indices such as skin conductance level. Related to sweating and the temperature of the skin, several measures are available which all depend on passing a small current through the skin (e.g. between fingers) and seeing how much the current is changed by its passage. Variously named *skin conductance* or *skin resistance level* (SCL/SRL), *galvanic skin response* (GSR) or *electrodermal activity* (EDA), these measures are very quick and simple, and have formed a large part of the biofeedback market through simple "relaxometers" which can be used almost anywhere. Of course, by their very nature these measures are somewhat limited. Calibration is a problem since levels will change over time independent of arousal. Furthermore, different environmental conditions, body temperatures and circadian rhythms will all mitigate against comparisons across settings. Nevertheless, some useful applications are possible; for example, this approach was used to good effect by Schmid and Peper (1987), who were able to demonstrate arousal–performance relationships using *finger temperatures* of Olympic rhythmic gymnasts. Higher temperatures immediately prior to performance were associated with worse performance. Of course, this is a rather simple finding, especially given the ways in which arousal/anxiety theories have moved on since. However, given the limitations imposed by such major competitions (in the Olympics for example, nothing can be attached to, nor make contact with, the athlete), such approaches would seem to be one of the only ways in which highly desirable and ecologically valid data can be collected.

The major problem relating to these measures is the high assumed, but practically almost negligible, interrelationship apparent between the different indices.

Even as recently as the mid 1980s, many subscribed to the idea of a unidimensional arousal construct (Duffy, 1962), under which all indices went up or down in parallel patterns depending on the level of activation in the system. In fact, investigations have increasingly supported Lacey's multidimensional theory (Lacey, 1967), which predicts that different measures co-vary; i.e. under increased arousal some go up whilst others decrease. In short, the picture is a lot more complex than was once thought. For example, as far as EMG is concerned, anxiety-induced arousal is associated with bursts of activity rather than general increases in tone (Fridlund, Hatfield, Cottam, & Fowler, 1986). A propos of EEG, as later sections will show, a simple "brain quiescence" interpretation of alpha rhythm has fortunately also been superseded (Petsche, Pockberger & Rappelsberger, 1988; Shaw 1996). Research has also identified reasonably stable gender differences related to how stress is experienced (e.g. Martinez-Selva, Gomez-Amor, Olmos, Navaro, & Roman, 1987), a finding which fits well with the hereditary view of stress responsivity which can, in turn, relate to a wide variety of psychological traits such as sensation-seeking behaviour (cf. Fahrenberg, 1986). In fact, there are even stable individual variations in how well the various indices are perceived (Steptoe & Vogele, 1992), so the choice of index for arousal-related investigations or biofeedback interventions is a somewhat sticky one!

In summary, examination of arousal/relaxation states using psychophysiological techniques is still extremely effective, although care must be taken to select an appropriate index, both for the situation and the subject. In fact, developments within sport psychology have switched the focus from simply arousal per se to pre-performance emotional state and, more specifically, how attention is allocated in this crucial phase.

Pre-performance Emotion and Activity

As mentioned earlier, the comparatively non-invasive nature of psychophysiological studies makes them ideal for the examination of preparative states and activities in real time and in ecologically valid settings. Therefore, building from the ideas of more global states related to excitation level, psychophysiological investigations have moved towards a more mechanistic focus, inferring both mental/emotional state and cognitive/meta-cognitive activity from physiological measures. In this respect, almost all of the indices mentioned in the previous section can be modified for employment. Thus, in a series of investigations, Hanin has employed a variety of peripheral measures of excitation, in combination with self-perceived ratings collected across a large number of performances, in order to tease out a "Zone of Optimal Function" (ZOF) for each individual athlete (Hanin & Syrja, 1995).

However, central measures are obviously optimum for examination of this situation because, interpretation problems notwithstanding, they offer the most direct focus on the processes of interest. EEG has formed the bulk of this thrust. Many investigations still focus on "the ubiquitous alpha rhythm" as the variable of interest. However, others have extended the search to encompass comparatively new higher-frequency signals (gamma, for example), and it will be interesting to see where these investigations lead.

In sports settings, EEG is collected by surface electrodes attached to specific areas of the scalp so as to overlie known areas of the brain. This is known as the 10–20 system because it divides the scalp into sections using units of 10% or 20% of the distance between two pairs of landmarks—the two ears in one direction and the top of the nose (nasion) to the lump on the back of the skull (inion) for the other (Jasper, 1958). Accordingly, temporal sites (on the temples!) have the prefix "T", central sites (overlying the central cortex) "C", visual cortex (occipital) "O" and so on. Odd numbers represent sites on the left of the skull, even to the right, with the actual number relating to where on the head the site is located. Recordings of activity are usually taken constantly, with signals digitised and stored for subsequent analysis, although real-time analysis is available (and essential for biofeedback applications). Accordingly, digitising issues commented on earlier must be catered for, and the sampling rates at which the analogue signal is coded and stored will be key to the subsequent veracity of findings. In the post-hoc analysis which typifies sport psychophysiology applications, the total signal, already filtered, is split into sections of time called epochs, and then examined by reference to predetermined frequency bands, in order to identify the quantity or power of activity in each band as a part of the total signal. A typical approach uses Fast Fourier Transform (FFT), a mathematical algorithm which also imposes certain requirements on the sampling rate and nature of the data. Generally, sampling rates must be high (>128 Hz) and epochs must be reasonably long (>1 s) if artefactual signals are to be avoided. The resulting data, and indeed the waveform itself, are referred to as *background EEG* in order to avoid confusion with the more complex research tool known as *evoked potentials* (EP). The EP methodology averages signals over many trials in order to tease out the specific potential evoked by a stimulus, which represents the only consistent feature of the environment. This approach represents a very powerful research tool, but is of little value in biofeedback and thus will not be considered further. Suffice to say that background EEG represents the ongoing activity of the brain at a particular time, and hence only some of the signals recorded will be due to the specific stimulus of interest. Thus, for example, the golfer's cerebral activity will reflect his or her thinking about the putt. Additionally, however, mental activity related to maintaining stance, wondering what to have for lunch, in fact a broad gamut of thought-related activity will also be present and detected by the examination of EEG, albeit that some activities will result in signals from specific sites. Accordingly, the trick in background EEG is to ensure that the subject is focused on the stimulus of interest, with distractions minimised, in order that activity may be ascribed to that particular event.

In the main, EEG alpha has been used as an index of visual attention (see the next section) but also, specific to emotion, as an indicator for self-talk when detected at specific sites. One of the most robust findings in sport psychophysiology, at least from a group data perspective, is the association between left hemisphere alpha (8- to 13-Hz activity from sites on the left of the brain) and good performance in a variety of sports, including target sports (e.g. shooting: Hatfield, Landers, & Ray, 1984; archery: Landers, Petruzello, Salazar, Crews, Kubitz, Gannon, & Han, 1991), golf (Crews & Landers, 1993), karate (Collins, Powell, & Davies, 1990), soccer penalty taking (Collins, Powell, & Davies, 1991) and weight lifting (Gannon, 1991). However, the apparently simple causative relationship between left hemisphere alpha and performance is, perhaps not surprisingly, far more complex than at first sight. The essential step of interpretation (cf. earlier sections) does offer some assistance, however. T3 and C3′ (temporal and central sites on the left side of the head) are both close to two well-established areas of the cerebral cortex known to be involved in dialogue, namely Broca's area and Wernicke's area (see Kolb & Wishaw, 1995). Self-talk in these circumstances is usually associated with negative emotion—the athlete talking to him- or herself about the consequences of failure, or trying to convince himself or herself that this will not occur. Thus the interpretation "greater self-talk (and hence less alpha) = lower performance", an idea originally proposed by Hatfield et al. (1984), even though the picture is probably more complex (Loze, Holmes, Collins, Shaw, & Bellamy, in review), may well be the causative interpretation which offers the way forwards. Once again, consideration of psychophysiology data in combination with self-report and performance biofeedback would seem to be the correct course of action.

In summary, pre-performance emotional state and activity can be effectively and efficiently evaluated by peripheral measures. However, the resulting information may inform only that, say, athlete A performs best in this state, but offers little about the ways in which this state affects performance or even how best this state may be achieved. The use of more central indices, which relate more directly to the factors that may "cause" the performance, offers both a mechanism for the effect of pre-performance state on outcome and also some good clues as to a possible solution.

In-Performance Activity and Attention

As mentioned earlier, the emphasis of psychophysiology has swung away from a pre-occupation with levels of arousal and excitation towards a focus on in-event mental activity. For a variety of reasons, this focus has largely considered aspects of attention; specifically, how it is allocated and to which factors. Once again, more central measures have been most useful, and the excellent temporal resolution of the background EEG, in particular its ability to highlight changes in activity across time, has been a prime technique in this respect.

In a typical intervention addressing this area, Landers and colleagues (1991) used biofeedback to either increase (the desired pattern) or decrease (for experimental purposes) left hemisphere alpha activity in novice archers. The intervention certainly worked—the archers who received the "increase" feedback increased alpha power and improved performance, whilst the other group lowered both alpha power and performance! This was a very good study with obvious implications for applied sport psychologists. However, underlying explanations for the meaning of increased left hemisphere power have varied from decreased self-talk (cf. the previous section), through lowered arousal levels (cf. the section before that), to the use of a more spatially appropriate, hemispherically specialised cognitive style.

This section of the chapter explores some of these explanations in more detail. This is done to provide another exemplar of the interpretation process which is so essential to effective psychophysiology. Additionally, however, especially since at least three competing explanations of alpha have been offered in this chapter already, it does seem that a more unifying explanation for the effects seen may be useful, and preferably one which is based on the primary significance of the alpha rhythm as indicating a resting or quiescent state for the visual cortex. One such explanation, which offers a good example of the way in which interpretation of signal can impact on the use of biofeedback and other mental skills, is the concept of *intention*—a term coined by Wertheim (1981) and extended in sport-relevant contexts by Shaw (1996).

The basic idea underlying intention is that increased levels of power in the alpha band are associated with less utilisation of retinal feedback in oculomotor and associated control. In other words, when alpha levels are high in sport settings, it is likely that the individual is controlling movements through reference to a stored model or internal representation rather than the active processing of concurrent visual information. Both Wertheim (1981) and a later replication by Loze, Collins, and Shaw (1999) have shown that visual tracking of predicable movement patterns results in higher levels of alpha than tracking same size but less predictable patterns. Data from Loze et al. (1999), presented in Figures 2.4 and 2.5, demonstrate this effect. Note that this effect is most marked at occipital sites (O1, O2); not really surprising as these sites overlie the visual cortex which, as previous sections stated, is the area that provides the genesis of the alpha rhythm. However, this visually based interpretation has important implications for the sports which have used biofeedback on EEG, almost all

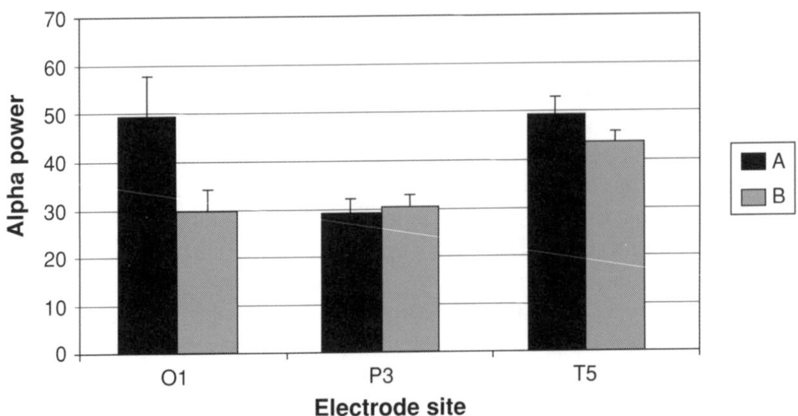

Figure 2.4 Mean alpha power ($\mu v \times \mu v$) at left hemisphere sites associated with visual tracking of a predictable (A) and an unpredictable (B) target. (From Loze et al., 1999, by permission)

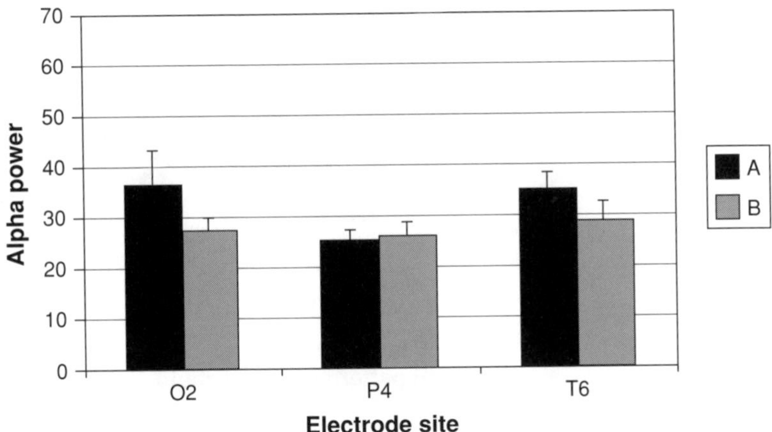

Figure 2.5 Mean alpha power ($\mu v \times \mu v$) at right hemisphere sites associated with visual tracking of a predictable (A) and an unpredictable (B) target

of which involve some form of target accuracy. If we subscribe to this interpretation (and readers may like to consider this explanation against the brief data presented in Chapter 4), greater alpha and better performance may be associated with less active processing of visual information just preceding performance. Thus, in the last few seconds before trigger pull, athletes would exhibit a switch from attention to intention (i.e. from external visual focus on the target to internal focus on the programme to enable a smooth trigger pull), which is the factor associated with good performance. In fact, this explanation makes very good sense when placed against self-report data from target sport athletes and coaches, who stress the need to "avoid forcing the sight picture" and "feel relaxed and open" in the final phase of the shot. Subscription to this explanation enables the practitioner to lock the biofeedback in with a whole range of different mental skills, all aimed at increasing the likelihood of the switch to a low cognition and highly automatic intentive state at the end of the aim.

The point is that the intention state offers a clear and consistent explanation for observed effects that also fits with what athletes and coaches believe is going on. Of course they may be wrong, and data in Chapter 4 hopefully demonstrate the limited scope of their accuracy. Once again, however, the need for interpretation through recourse to mechanisms and the utility of triangulation of different data emerge as features of good practice.

Other psychophysiological indices are also used as markers of attention. Firstly, several of the measures already identified earlier, such as phasic HR changes through IBI (cf. Boutcher & Zinsser, 1990), are used as indicators of increases in an internally orientated attentive focus. In an interesting new development, we are increasingly using personalised profiles rather than the group-based data sets which have typified work to date. More akin to the "zone of optimal function" ideas of Hanin, this approach represents the logical conclusion of triangulating data between physiological indices,

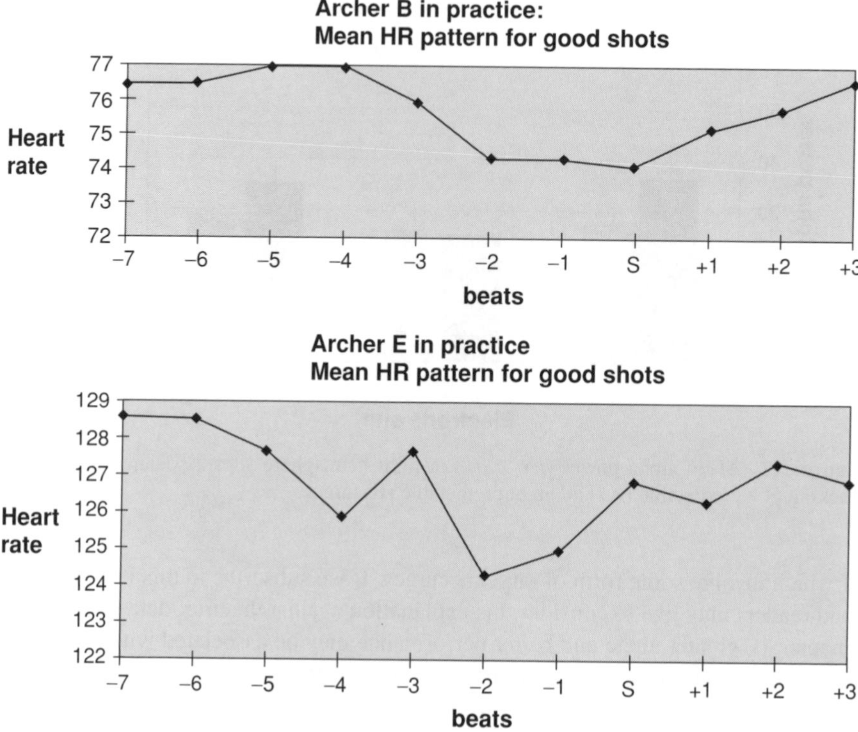

Figure 2.6 Variations in IBI profiles for archers during varying conditions of good shots, from 7 beats before (−7) to 3 beats after (+3) arrow release. (Data from Bellamy, Collins, Holmes, & Loze, 1999)

self-reported mental activity and outcome measures. Thus, in Figure 2.6 for example, two very distinct patterns are apparent. Archer B exhibits a profile very much like the group effects described by Boutcher and Zinsser, whilst archer E is a lot more variable. The point for this chapter is that psychophysiology may well need to take a much more individualised look in future, and this point is substantiated empirically in Chapter 4. Obviously, however, this approach is entirely consistent with biofeedback, which has always been based largely on individual profiles.

Finally, the use of *Electro-oculography* or EOG must be described. EOG recordings are often taken to guard against artefacts in EEG from eye blinks and eye movement. However, EOG emerges as a measure in its own right, offering some clues as to eye movements associated with visual search, which is a useful adjunct to the central EEG data from the visual cortex. Some units use EOG from the muscles surrounding the eye to determine both broad movement patterns and more detailed gaze direction data. Increasingly, however, the latter is provided by specific *eye mark recorders*, which use a prismatic system to offer a camera view of exactly where the subject is looking. Whilst not a psychophysiological technique, this approach is increasingly used in tandem with such measures and is included here for completeness. In either case, gaze data offer useful information, especially in cases when gaze is disrupted through, for example, pre-performance anxiety. One limitation of eye mark recorders is that they focus attention (no pun intended) on foveal vision (the exact optical focus of the eye) as opposed to peripheral vision which, although much more difficult to examine, appears to be the preferred modality of expert performers. By contrast, allocation of attention to peripheral stimuli can be extrapolated from EOG data, albeit only when some fairly horrendous calibration problems have been addressed.

Muscle Activity and Skill Acquisition

This final applications section gives us the opportunity for a slightly more in-depth look at *EMG*. Electromyographic recordings can be taken with intramuscular needle electrodes. Unsurprisingly, however, this is not a popular option and the vast majority of sport-related studies use surface electrodes. Most of the issues affecting this modality have already been covered. Electrodes are almost always sited along the body of the muscle in question, with locations one-third and two-thirds along the length being the norm. As mentioned earlier, small pre-amplifiers are often used in order to improve signal-to-noise ratios, especially since telemetry (radio transmission) of signals is increasingly used in order to maintain ecologically valid movement patterns.

Once the signal is filtered and amplified, some form of rectification of the signal is usually applied. As with other indices, examination of the raw signal waveform is interesting but offers little in the way of empirically analysable data. Accordingly, and since the signal is made up of both positive and negative potentials (above and below the line as per Figure 2.2), signals may be rectified by either ignoring all negative signals or reversing their polarity so that all signals are positive. Further signal conditioning may involve totalling activity across a regular time base, resetting counters to zero in order to provide an integrated signal.

Analysis may look at amplitude or, more rarely, frequency. Increasingly, however, signal patterns are compared across two or more conditions. Thus, investigators may contrast "at rest" with active patterns, or use an increase from baseline measure, or contrast signals obtained under different execution conditions such as variations in speed. Subsequent treatments of data are increasingly complex, with the application of spectral analysis techniques to tease out underlying trends or collective patterns in the data. In this way, EMG data are making a full contribution to the comparatively new approaches within motor control, such as dynamical systems.

It should be noted that biofeedback has received a new lease of "sporting life" via its increasing application to the development of technical expertise. EMG biofeedback is increasingly used to aid the development and fine tuning of technique, especially when an optimum pattern has been identified. Thus, for example, Krueger, Ruehl, Scheel, and Franz (1988) used EMG biofeedback to optimise technique with the new "wing" Kayak paddle, by encouraging greater use of the latissimus dorsi, the "wing" muscles on the back. These interdisciplinary approaches, which draw substantially from both motor learning and biomechanics, represent an exciting new direction, and investigations aimed at identification of the most efficacious protocols for such interventions are highly desirable.

One final word is pertinent for all applications, and this relates to the optimum use of psychophysiology in field settings as well as, or even in preference to, laboratory based investigations. I have already highlighted the considerable benefits of using such an ecologically valid investigative technique. To fully exploit these advantages, however, it is essential to recognise the large differences which may exist between laboratory and field measures. Differences are substantial, with often little or no relationship apparent between measures taken in the two settings (see e.g. Fahrenburg, Foerster, Schneider, & Muller, 1986; Marstaller & Meischner, 1990). Accordingly, one must be cautious of psychophysiological data which have been collected in low-fidelity situations, i.e. where either little ecological validity is apparent or where no checks of subject perceptions have been made. A good example from our own work was the decision not to use EOG electrodes with pistol shooters and archers, even though this has been commonly reported in the literature. All participants reported such high levels of discomfort with these "non-usual" measures that we felt the resulting data might well be questionable. Such decisions are hard to take, and "best fit" compromises may frequently be necessary. Investigators must try to maximise reality in testing settings, however, especially if consequent data are to form the basis of an applied, biofeedback-based intervention. Mainstream psychophysiology is increasingly recognising the strengths inherent in the use of field settings and data assessed via ambulatory techniques, especially for the examination of clinical problems (Turpin, 1990). The advantages of sport psychology as an applied discipline must not be cast aside in the interests of the greater academic respectability perceived to be afforded by laboratory designs.

FEEDBACK SYSTEMS: CONSCIOUS CHANGE VERSUS AUTOMATICITY

One final brief word is necessary about the third stage of the biofeedback model proposed in Figure 2.1, namely the modality and style of the feedback itself. An increasing volume of anecdotal and empirical data, including much from my own laboratory and applied work, attests to the need for highly automatic, low-conscious thought-related control in competitive sports settings (Collins, Morriss, Bellamy, & Hooper, in review; Jones & Collins, 1996; Morriss & Bartlett, 1996; Newell & Corcos, 1993). Accordingly, there is a potentially delicate balance to be struck between the consciously mediated control which is a feature of biofeedback interventions, especially in the early stages, and the automaticity which may need to be a feature of the eventual execution of the learnt response. For example, would a visual display for the biofeedback data inhibit or disrupt, say, a key visual feature of task execution? If so, then auditory feedback is indicated, although even here some inhibition by conscious thought may result. This is a minor but potentially significant problem that must be considered in any such work.

Used correctly, however, with appropriate checks to guard against some of these potential pitfalls, biofeedback is obviously an extremely useful tool for applied work with athletes. Sensible procedures will ensure that benefits are optimised and, in this respect, the five-step approach to mental training described by Blumenstein, Bar-Eli, and Tenenbaum (1997) offers an excellent aide-memoire. Of particular merit is their recognition that practitioners need to "identify and strengthen the most efficient biofeedback modality" (p. 450). If such procedures are used with full cognizance of the concerns outlined in this chapter, effective and permanent performance gains can be made.

REFERENCES

Bellamy, M. B., Collins, D., Holmes, P., & Loze, G. (1999). Shot patterns in ECG recordings for elite air-pistol shooters. *Journal of Sports Sciences*, **17**, 48–49.

Blumenstein, B., Bar-Eli, M., & Tenenbaum, G. (1997). A five-step approach to mental training incoroporating biofeedback. *The Sport Psychologist*, **11**, 440–453.

Boutcher, S. H., & Zinnser, N. W. (1990). Cardiac deceleration of elite and beginning golfers during putting. *Journal of Sport and Exercise Psychology*, **12**, 37–47.

Cacioppo, J. Y., & Tassinary, L. G. (eds.) (1990). *Principles of psychophysiology: Physical, social and inferential elements*. Cambridge: Cambridge University Press.

Collins, D. J., Powell, G. E., & Davies, I. (1990). An electro-encephalographic study of hemispheric processing patterns during karate performance. *Journal of Sport and Exercise Psychology*, **12**, 223–234.

Collins, D. J., Powell, G. E., & Davies, I. (1991). Cerebral activity prior to motion task performance: An electroencephalographic study. *Journal of Sports Science*, **9**, 313–324.

Collins, D., Morriss, C., Bellamy, M., & Hooper, H. (1997). Competition stress effects on kinematics and performance level in elite javelin throwers. *Journal of Applied Sport Psychology*, **9**, S38.

Crews, D. J., & Landers, D. M. (1993). Electroencephalographic measures of attentional patterns prior to the golf putt. *Medicine and Science in Sports and Exercise*, **25**, 116–126.

Donchin, E., & Coles, M. G. H. (1988). On the conceptual foundations of cognitive psychophysiology. *The Behavioral and Brain Sciences*, **11**, 408–419.

Duffy, E. (1962). *Activation and behavior*. New York: Wiley.

Fahrenberg, J. (1986). Psychophysiological individuality: A pattern analytic approach to personality research and psychosomatic medicine. *Advances in Behavioural Research and Therapy*, **8**, 43–100.

Fahrenburg, J., Foerster, F., Schneider, H.-J., & Muller, W. (1986). Predictability of individual differences in activation processes in a field setting based on laboratory measures. *Psychophysiology*, **23**, 323–333.

Fenz, W. D., & Epstein, S. (1967). Gradients of physiological arousal of experienced and novice parachutists as a function of an approaching jump. *Psychosomatic Medicine*, **29**, 33–51.

Fridlund, A. J., Hatfield, M. E., Cottam, G. L., & Fowler, S. C. (1986). Anxiety and striate-muscle activation: Evidence from electromyographic pattern analysis. *Journal of Abnormal Psychology*, **95**, 228–236.

Gannon, T. L. (1991). *An analysis of temporal EEG patterning prior to initiation of the arm curl*. University of Oregon: Microform Publications.

Hanin, E. G., & Syrja, P. (1995). Performance affect in junior ice hockey players: An application of the Individual Zones of Optimal Functioning Model. *The Sport Psychologist*, **9**, 169–187.

Hatfield, B. D., Landers, D. M., & Ray, W. J. (1984). Cognitive processes during self-paced motor performance: An electro-encephalographic profile of skilled marksmen. *Journal of Sport Psychology*, **6**, 42–59.

Jasper, (1958). Report of the committee on methods of clinical examination in electroencephalography. *Electroencephalography and Clinical Neurophysiology*, **10**, 370–375.

Jones, B. & Collins, D. J. (1996). Performance intervention for effective technical change: a case study. *Journal of Sports Sciences*, **14**, 33–34.

Kolb, B. & Wishaw, I. Q. (1995). *Fundamentals of human neuropsychology*. New York: W. H. Freeman & Co.

Krueger, K. M., Ruehl, M., Scheel, D., & Franz, U. (1988). Die Anwendbarkeit von EMG Biofeedback zur Optimierung sportlicher Techniken im motorischen Lernprozess von Ausdauersportarten am Beispiel des Kanurennsports. *Theorie und Praxis Leistungssport* (Leipzig), **26**, 128–142.

Lacey, J. I., & Lacey, B. C. (1970). Some autonomic-central nervous system interrelationship. In P. Black (ed.), *Physiological correlates of emotion*. New York: Academic Press.

Lacey, J. I. (1967). Somatic response patterning and stress: Some revisions of activation theory. In M. H. Appley & R. Trumbull (eds.), *Psychological stress*. New York: Century Crofts.

Landers, D. M., Petruzzello, S. J., Salazar, W., Crews, D. L., Kubitz, K. A., Gannon, T. L., & Han, M. (1991). The influence of electrocortical biofeedback on performance in pre-elite archers. *Medicine and Science in Sports and Exercise*, **23**, 123–129.

Loze, G. M., Collins, D. & Shaw, J. C. (1999). EEG alpha rhythm, intention and oculomotor control. *The International Journal of Psychophysiology*, **33**, 163–167.

Loze, G. M., Holmes, P., Collins, D., Shaw, J. C., & Bellamy, M. J. B. (In review). Examining the neuropsychological mechanisms underlying UIT air-pistol shooting performance. *International Journal of Sport Psychology.*

Marstaller, H., & Meischner, K. (1990, June). *The predictability of psychophysical states (laboratory-field comparison)*. Paper presented at the 19th annual meeting of the German Psychophysiology Society (DGPA), University of Giessen.

Martinez-Selva, J. M, Gomez-Amor, J., Olmos, E., Navaro, N., & Roman, F. (1987). Sex and menstrual cycle differences in the habituation and spontaneous recovery of the electrodermal orienting reaction. *Personality and Individual Differences*, **8**, 211–217.

Morriss, C. J., & Bartlett, R. M. (1996). Biomechanical factors critical for performance in the men's javelin throw. *Sports Medicine*, **21**, 438–446.

Newell, K. M., & Corcos, D. M. (1993). *Variability and motor control*. Champaign, IL; Human Kinetics.

Obrist, P. A., Howard, J. L., Lawler, J. E., Galosy, R. A., Meyers, K. A., & Gaelein, C. J. (1974). The cardiac-somatic interaction. In P. A. Obrist, A. H. Black, & L. V. DiCara (eds.), *Cardiovascular psychophysiology*. Chicago: Alsine.

Petsche, H., Pockberger, H., & Rappelsberger, P. (1988). EEG topography and mental performance. In F. H. Duffy (ed.), *Topographic mapping of brain electrical activity* (pp. 63–98). London: Butterworths.

Salazar, W., Landers, D. M., Petruzzello, S. J., Han, M., Crews, D. L., & Kubitz, K. A. (1990). Hemispheric asymmetry, cardiac response and performance in elite archers. *Research Quarterly for Exercise and Sport*, **61**, 351–359.

Schmid, A. B., & Peper, E. (1987). Psychological readiness states of the top 1984 rhythmic gymnasts. In J. H. Salmela, B. Petoit, & T. B. Hoshizaki (eds.), *Psychological nurturing and guidance of gymnastic talent.* Montreal: Sport Psyche Editions.

Shaw, J. C., 1996. Intention as a component of the alpha-rhythm response to mental activity. *International Journal of Psychophysiology*, **24**, 7–23.

Smith, N. J., & Collins, D. J. (1991). *The role of psychophysiology as a research and intervention tool in sport psychology*. Paper presented at the annual meeting of the British Psychophysiology Society. Birkbeck College, London, September.

Steptoe, A., & Vogele, C. (1992). Individual differences in the perception of bodily sensations: The role of trait anxiety and coping style. *Behavioural Research Therapy*, **30**, 597–607.

Turpin, G. (1990). Ambulatory clinical psychophysiology: An introduction to techniques and methodological issues. *Journal of Psychophysiology*, **4**, 299–304.

Wang, M. Q., & Landers, D. M. (1987). *Cardiac responses and hemispheric differentiation during archery performance: A psychophysiological investigation of attention.* Unpublished manuscript, Arizona State University.

Wertheim, A. H. (1981). Occipital alpha activity as a measure of retinal involvement in oculomotor control. *Psychophysiology*, **18**, 432–439.

Zani, A., & Rossi, B. (1991). Cognitive psychophysiology as an interface between cognitive and sport psychology. *International Journal of Sport Psychophysiology*, **22**, 376–398.

CHAPTER 3

Biofeedback Applications in Sport and Exercise: Research Findings

Boris Blumenstein

INTRODUCTION

The main purpose of this chapter is to describe the current state of applied biofeedback research, not only in sport, but also in clinical practice, which has been previously discussed in various books (Andreassy, 2000; Basmajian & Wolf, 1990), reviews (Blumenstein & Bar-Eli, 2001; Collins, 1995), and studies (Blumenstein, Bar-Eli, & Tenenbaum, 1995, 1997b; Caird, McKenzie & Sleivert, 1999). Biofeedback in sport has been used to enhance athlete performance, as a technique for teaching athletes to deal with general and specific anxiety, to reduce pain and fatigue, and to increase flexibility. This chapter will begin by explaining the term "biofeedback modalities" and by briefly outlining the history of research on this topic. Next, several studies in biofeedback applications in sport and exercise will be reviewed and evaluated, such as biofeedback and reducing anxiety; biofeedback and improving muscle performance; and biofeedback and improving athletic performance. In addition, studies that use biofeedback as part of a large multifaceted treatment program will be evaluated, and, more specifically, papers that have investigated the effects of biofeedback in different sport disciplines will be reviewed.

BIOFEEDBACK MODALITIES

A major application for biofeedback is detecting and helping in the management of psychophysiological arousal, especially overarousal. The main physiological processes commonly associated with overarousal within the field of biofeedback include skeletal muscle tension, peripheral vasoconstriction (smooth muscle activity), and

Brain and Body in Sport and Exercise: Biofeedback Applications in Performance Enhancement.
Edited by Boris Blumenstein, Michael Bar-Eli, and Gershon Tenenbaum.

electrodermal activity. These three (especially the first two) are the most common biofeedback modalities (Peek, 1987).

"Biofeedback modalities" refers to the various types of instrumentation used for physiological signal recording and for feedback. Several biofeedback modalities have been used in sport, such as the measurement of muscle tension by electromyography (muscle feedback, EMG), the measurement of peripheral skin temperature as an index of peripheral blood flow (thermal feedback, often referred to as "temperature," Temp), the measurement of electrodermal or sweat gland activity (electrodermal feedback, EDA), the measurement of the brain's electrical activity (electroencephalographic feedback, EEG), the measurement of heart activity by electrocardiography, including heart rate [cardiovascular or heart rate (HR) feedback and blood pressure (BP) feedback]. Among these modalities, biofeedback training with EMG, EDA, and HR (recently with EEG) has been used more intensively to improve athletes' performance via psychoregulation in various sport disciplines. For example, nearly 60% of the studies reviewed by Zaichkowsky and Fuchs (1988) that examined the effect of EMG biofeedback reported positive effects on performance. However, the reviews of Petruzzello, Landers, and Salazar (1991) and Collins (1995) showed performance-enhancing effects by HR, respiration, and slow potentials (SPs) biofeedback. While the interest of biofeedback researchers in sport has recently shifted somewhat towards the identification of psychological conditions associated with better performance, particularly in closed skill sports, the modification of athletes' arousal states via biofeedback is still of great interest to coaches, athletes, and applied sport psychologists (Collins, 1995; Zaichkowsky & Takenaka, 1993) (see below).

Muscle or Electromyographic Feedback

Measurement of the electrical activity preceding muscle contraction is called electromyography or EMG. EMG measures (in microvolts) the electrical energy discharged by the motor nerve endings signaling a muscle to contract.

Generally, in EMG biofeedback, surface electrodes [usually three silver/silver chloride electrodes: two active and one reference (ground)] are attached to the prepared skin and the electrical activity of the target muscle(s) is shown to the subject, either visually or auditorily or both. In sport psychology practice, the selection of electrode sites for various muscle groups must be very carefully considered. Many variations are possible, and the user may find one of these variations more applicable than others to his/her particular situation (Basmajian, 1983; Schwartz, 1987). Usually, frontal muscle activity is a valid indicator of general arousal and muscle tension (Zaichkowsky & Fuchs, 1988), a general "barometer" of muscular tension throughout the head and upper neck regions. In our research and practical work (Blumenstein, Bar-Eli, & Tenenbaum,1995, 1997a), we placed the surface EMG electrodes on the frontalis (forehead) muscle, following Kondo, Canter, and Bean (1977). The ground electrode may conveniently be placed between the two active electrodes. The EMG was measured using averaged peak-to-peak microvoltage (p-p μV) values of EMG activity for determined sample times.

One of the common aims in EMG biofeedback application is to evaluate the efficacy of EMG biofeedback training; that is, to verify that a mastery of self-regulation has been achieved for a given criterion. Several researchers (Blumenstein, Bar-Eli, & Tenenbaum, 1995, 1997a; Zaichkowsky & Fuchs, 1986) have proposed approximate guidelines, summarized as follows:

1. A reading on the frontal muscle of 2–5 μV indicates that the monitored muscle is not relaxed.
2. A reading on the frontal muscle of 1–2 μV shows that the muscle tension is "normal," although deeper levels of relaxation can be obtained.
3. A reading on the frontal muscle below 1 μV indicates that the muscle is quite relaxed, and below 0.6 μV it is very relaxed.

Likewise, there are several important questions in EMG biofeedback applications for which there are no clear answers, among them: For how long and how quickly must one be able to lower or raise EMG activity (for example, in our approach athletes can change their EMG activity to 0.6μV during 1 min)? How many EMG training sessions must be held? For example, Nielsen and Holmes (1980) reported that a minimum of 4 × 20-min forehead EMG treatment sessions should be held to achieve a relaxation state.

Many biofeedback training sessions are reported in the literature to last only 16, 10, or even 3 min (Shellenberger & Green, 1986). In our research and practice, we use EMG training together with relaxation and imagery. This usually lasts about 20 min, during which the athlete is connected to the EMG feedback system and is able to fulfill the task of controlling EMG level (more details in Blumenstein, Bar-Eli, & Tenenbam, 1995, 1997a). We therefore urge researchers to consider these questions in future efficacy studies.

Thermal Feedback

The next feedback modality in use is thermal feedback (often called "temperature," Temp). This feedback, most often in the form of audio and/or visual signals which reflect temperature changes (usually skin temperature fluctuations of the fingers and hands), provides information on the peripheral circulation.

The cardiovascular mechanisms that regulate skin temperature in the hands are closely related to the activity of the sympathetic division of the autonomic nervous system. When this system is activated, the smooth muscles surrounding the blood vessels near the skin surface are likely to contract, resulting in vasoconstriction. This will cause a decrease in the flow of blood in the area. Decreasing quantities of blood flowing through the tissues near the skin surface will bring about a drop in skin temperature. Conversely, an increase in hand temperature is accompanied by vasodilation (a relaxation of the smooth muscles surrounding the peripheral blood vessels in the hands) and results from the relaxation of sympathetic activity. According to Zaichkowsky and Fuchs (1988), the values of peripheral skin temperature range from 18–21 °C (high sympathetic arousal) to 32–35 °C (low sympathetic arousal). Temperature biofeedback is usually used in conjunction with other modalities (Goodspeed, 1983; Zaichkowsky & Fuchs, 1988), for example with electrodermal biofeedback (see below). In addition, skin temperature biofeedback with electrodermal or muscle biofeedback is used together and in conjunction with other relaxation techniques to initiate a relaxation response that might be used to combat precompetition anxiety (Peper & Schmid, 1983) or stage fright (Kamimura & Kodama, 1995). Moreover, temperature biofeedback is often used in gymnastics (Goodspeed, 1983; Peper & Schmid, 1983) and winter sports (Kappers & Chapman, 1984).

Electrodermal Feedback

Two of the more fascinating feedback modalities that have inspired voluminous research over the last 100 years are concerned with the electrical activity of the skin. According to Peek (1987), it is not clear how one would easily determine whether a sweat gland was "on," how much sweat was being secreted, or how many such glands were active. However, since sweat contains salts that make it electrically conductive, sweaty skin is more conductive to electricity than dry skin. Hence, skin conductance activity (SCA) corresponds well to sweat gland activity. This, along with other electrical properties of the skin, is known as electrodermal activity (EDA) and has historically been known as "galvanic skin response" (GSR). According to Peek (1987), GSR has been recognized as a way to gain objective access to psychophysiological arousal. Electrical conductance increases with skin moisture because current flows more easily through the salty moisture on the skin surface, and conductivity decreases as moisture decreases. Biofeedback instruments have been developed that monitor various aspects of this physiological activity. A skin conductance device applies a very small electrical pressure (voltage) to the skin, typically on the volar surface of the fingers or the palmar surface of the hand (where there are many sweat glands), and measures the amount of electrical current that the skin will allow to pass. EDA has been recognized as distinctively sensitive to transitory emotional states and mental events, while often remaining more or less independent of other biofeedback measures such as muscle tension and skin temperature.

EDA and skin temperature biofeedback may be used together (Zaichkowsky & Fuchs, 1988) and in conjunction with other relaxation techniques to institute a relaxation response that might be used to combat precompetition anxiety (Goodspeed, 1983; Peper & Schmid, 1983). According to Zaichkowsky and Fuchs (1988), all studies that use temperature biofeedback as a treatment for athletic anxiety incorporate EDA biofeedback training as a mode to learn state anxiety control. It seems that complete training of the autonomic nervous system via biofeedback for anxiety reduction should include EDA biofeedback training for situational anxiety and temperature biofeedback training for reducing chronic "trait" anxiety (Zaichowsky & Fuchs, 1988).

People who have worked with skin conductance feedback (the modern term for GSR) are familiar with observing responses to emotional stimuli. However, it must be emphasized that these instruments measure sweat gland activity, and statements regarding skin conductance and emotionality (anxiety, fear, anger, and so forth) are inferences from one's own theoretical perspective and are not based upon the systematic collection of group data (Sandweiss, 1985). Skin conductance biofeedback is generally employed as a monitoring device during an interview targeted to the identification of stress factors.

Electroencephalography

The electroencephalogram, or EEG, is a complex bioelectric signal that reflects the functional status of large pools of cortical neurons and their modulation by subcortical regulatory influences. The interpretation of this signal requires a comprehensive knowledge of both the technical aspects of EEG recording and the neurophysiology of the central nervous system. Thus, the application of this modality in the biofeedback context must be conducted or supervised by a properly trained and experienced professional (Standards and Guidelines for Biofeedback Application, 1992).

The human brain produces a continuous output of minute electrical signals. The magnitude of these signals is so small that it is measured in microvolts (μV), or millionths of a volt. However, the signals can be accurately detected and recorded. To do this, the signals must first be picked up by electrodes attached to the surface of the scalp and then amplified and filtered many thousands of times before they can be analyzed. If these amplified signals are recorded by the tracing pens of an electroencephalograph, the record will appear as a continuous wave of varying frequency and amplitude—the EEG.

The number of EEG cycles occurring within a given time interval is called its frequency and is measured in hertz (Hz) or cycles per second (CPS). The greater the number of cycles per second, the higher the frequency. The EEG appears to contain four major frequency bands: beta (above 13 Hz), alpha (8–13 Hz), theta (4–7 Hz), and delta (0.5–3.5 Hz). An EEG is not useful for determining specific brain functions, but for discerning more general states of arousal, which are identified as: delta: deep sleep; theta: periods of dreaming; alpha: relaxed awareness; beta: full alertness (Walter, 1963).

According to Petruzzello et al. (1991), the spontaneous electrical activity of the brain, recorded at the scalp and referred to as EEG, can be broken down into numerous bandwidths based on frequency components. Perhaps the most frequently used bandwidth in biofeedback investigations has been the alpha bandwidth.

EEG feedback is an instrumental learning process whose end result is the facilitation of voluntary control of EEG activity. This procedure involves the use of external EEG monitoring devices especially designed to convey to the individual ongoing information concerning the electrical activity of his/her brain. For example, the athlete may hear a tone, the presence of which indicates the occurrence of EEG alpha activity of 20 μV or greater. He may recognize that whenever this tone appears, he coincidentally experiences a relaxed, "idling" mental state where he is not thinking about anything in particular. By sustaining this relaxed mental state he notices that the tone stays on for greater periods of time. If he loses his concentration and is unable to sustain the state the tone disappears. By observing the tone (feedback display) and the corresponding "mental set," the athlete learns to regulate subtle shifts in feeling and attention. He can do this because he is receiving ongoing feedback of the processes involved.

EEG biofeedback could affect athletic performance, specifically in target sports such as shooting, archery, and golf. For example, Hatfield, Landers, and Ray (1984) reported that as shooters prepare to shoot, there is a marked shift from left to right hemispheric activation. Crews (1991) found that for golf performance, the greater left-to-right hemisphere changes in EEG spectral densities paralleled those found in archery studies (Landers et al., 1991). A series of studies (Collins, Powell, & Davies, 1990, 1991) with karate, soccer, and cricket has demonstrated an increase in alpha band activity in both hemispheres. In addition, increases in temporal and central alpha power preceded success, and failure was associated with decreased alpha activity (Collins, 1995). Finally, the results of EEG biofeedback training on performance can determine the length of training programs and appropriate training criteria, and can be compared to other cognitive behavioral techniques to enhance performance.

Cardiovascular Feedback

Cardiovascular feedback has been used by researchers and clinicians to provide feedback about heart rate (HR). Control of the cardiovascular system via biofeedback training has been successful in clinical studies and sport. For example, studies in sport showed the possibility of decreasing the cardiovascular and respiratory effects of exercise by biofeedback training before and during the exercise regimen (e.g., Blumenstein, Breslav, Bar-Eli, Tenenbaum, & Weinstein, 1995). In addition, HR can be brought under voluntary control during both aerobic and anaerobic dynamic physical exercise (e.g., Perski, Tzankoff, & Engel, 1985). In other research HR was related to improved performance in aiming tasks (archery, shooting, golf putting) (Crews, 1991; Landers, 1985; Landers et al., 1991; Petruzzello et al., 1991), but HR biofeedback needs to be compared against other cognitive-behavioral techniques (e.g., relaxation, imagery, etc.; see Benson, Dryer, & Hartley, 1978; Blumenstein, Breslav, et al., 1995). Caird et al. (1999) reported on a study that attempts to determine whether a psychophysiological intervention of HR biofeedback and Jacobson's progressive muscular relaxation (Jacobson, 1938) could decrease the submaximal oxygen consumption ($VO_{2_{submax}}$) during treadmill running and improve running economy for a group of trained long-distance runners ($n = 7$ competitive runners). They found that the use of combined HR biofeedback and relaxation intervention improved running economy in the long-distance runners. Several studies found optimal HR zone in shooting (Landers, 1985) and ice hockey (Davis, 1991), using the special telemetry watch system (e.g., Polar Electro, Finland) to monitor HR responses of athletes between shots in shooting, while resting between shifts in hockey, etc. In addition, this portable HR biofeedback device may be used to teach athletes their optimal HR zone. Reductions in HR thought to result from HR biofeedback were found to be more closely related to respiratory factors (Petruzzello et al., 1991). HR variations may also be associated with biofeedback control of breathing pattern (De Pascalis, Anello, & Venturini, 1986; Hatch, Borchberding, & Norris, 1990).

Breathing pattern (depth and frequency of breathing) continually varies and is highly sensitive to changes of both arousal level and emotional factors (Mador & Tobin, 1991; Pack & McCool, 1992). Breathing rhythm, one of the oldest psychophysiological indices, was used mainly in psychopathological studies (Freedman, 1991; Peper & Schmid, 1983; Peper & Tibbetts, 1992). The fact that breathing pattern was rarely used in biofeedback studies in the realm of physical exercise may be related to methodological and technical difficulties or due to poor use of respiratory indices (Petruzzello et al., 1991; Sandweiss & Wolf, 1985). Blumenstein, Breslav, et al. (1995) found that, compared with HR, GSR, and EMG responses, breathing pattern is at least as sensitive to the mental techniques employed and may be useful as a psychophysiological tendency index for diagnosis and testing, especially in sport practice. We used breathing biofeedback training with elite athletes (e.g., swimming, archery, shooting) to decrease or increase levels of prestart physical stress in order to improve their performance (Blumenstein, 1996; Blumenstein, Tenenbaum, Bar-Eli, & Pie, 1995).

BIOFEEDBACK AND ANXIETY

According to Moran (1996), biofeedback training in sport psychology has been used most extensively in the treatment of performance anxiety. High levels of anxiety can be detrimental to motor learning, performance, and participation in competition (Martens, 1977). One way to build self-confidence and reduce competition anxiety is to improve performance skills. This can be accomplished over time by providing athletes with feedback on their skill improvement, effort, and, if warranted, their performance outcome (Anshel, 1995). An attempt to reduce state anxiety and improve balancing performance on a stabilometer was conducted in a study by Teague (1976). During four time sessions (each 60 min), both systematic desensitization and biofeedback (EMG) training were used, and it was found that 20 college students were able to reduce state anxiety and to improve balancing performance. Similar results were also reported by French (1978). The results showed that biofeedback (EMG) training significantly reduced general performance-debilitating muscle tension and improved balancing performance. In the Sabourin and Rioux (1979) study participants reduced tension and significantly improved their performance on the task after five biofeedback (EMG) training sessions (30 min each). Blais and Vallerand (1986) found that six biofeedback (EMG) training sessions (30 min each) improved balancing performance and reduced EMG tension.

Griffiths, Steel, Vaccaro, and Karpman (1981) and Zaichkowsky, Dorsey, and Mulholland (1979) examined the effects of biofeedback (EMG) training on reducing state anxiety and improving performance. The first study, reported by Griffiths et al. (1981), found a reduction in state anxiety after six biofeedback (EMG) and relaxation training sessions (each 20 min) but no significant improvement effect on performance. The second study, reported by Zaichkowsky et al. (1979), found that in six biofeedback (EMG) and systematic desensitization training sessions (each 15–20 min), there was no significant reduction in state anxiety or improvement in gymnastic performance. Similar results were also reported by Tsukomoto (1979) and by Weinberg and Hunt (1976). De Witt (1980) found a reduction in competitive stress and an improvement in football and basketball performance after biofeedback (EMG) training (football, 12 sessions × 30 min; basketball, 11 session × 60 min). The study by Daniels and Landers (1981) is perhaps the best example of creative biofeedback (HR, respiration) training being applied to help elite rifle shooters deal with performance anxiety.

The above studies indicate that biofeedback training effects (usually frontalis EMG) were not always successful in reducing anxiety and improving performance by reducing muscular tension. Moreover, other important factors in achieving these goals are the length of biofeedback treatment (sessions × time), performance tasks, combination of biofeedback training with other psychological techniques, and biofeedback modalities (usually frontal muscle activity, i.e., frontalis EMG).

BIOFEEDBACK AND MUSCLE PERFORMANCE

Improvement in muscle performance with biofeedback training (usually with EMG) is well-documented in clinical practice (Basmajian, 1983; Schwartz, 1987) and sport (Landers, 1988; Zaichkowsky & Fuchs, 1988). The practical application of biofeedback (EMG) training for increasing muscle strength was demonstrated by Lucca and Recchiuti (1983). After a 19-day program with biofeedback (EMG) training the experimental group showed significantly greater gains in average peak torque. In another study, Croce (1986) found that a training program of combined isokinetic exercise and biofeedback (EMG) training produced significant gains in maximal force and EMG activity of key extensor muscles. A study by Peper and Schmid (1983) demonstrated biofeedback (EMG, Temp, EDA) training effect on voluntary control over peripheral temperature, EMG activity, HR, and skin conductance of members of the US rhythmic gymnastics team.

Dorsey (1976) and Goodspeed (1983) found an improvement in gymnastics motor control and performance after biofeedback training programs (EMG and GSR, Temp). Ren (1995) reported a positive effect of biofeedback training (EMG) and demonstrated improved consistency of archers' muscle exerting from drawing to loosing, and thus enhanced postural consistency. Krueger, Ruehl, Scheel, and Franz (1988) used biofeedback training (EMG) to optimize technique with the new "wing" kayak paddle.

Some researchers have examined the effect of biofeedback training on muscle endurance and perceived pain. For example, Lloyd (1972) found that auditory biofeedback training with EMG did not significantly increase endurance time or decrease the degree of perceived pain. McGlynn, Laughlin, and Filios (1979) found significant reductions in the perceived mean pain level in a biofeedback (EMG) training group. Edwards and Lippold (1956) demonstrated that biofeedback (EMG) needs to be increased in order to sustain a given level of tension. This may indicate more efficiency in muscular contraction during the fatigue regimen (Middaugh, Miller, Foster, & Ferdon 1982).

The above studies indicate that biofeedback training attempted to increase muscle strength, and improve muscle control and induced muscle fatigue and pain. However, biofeedback training effects were not always successful. Biofeedback is generally considered an important tool for stress management and control, but it is usually quite difficult to demonstrate a direct relationship between biofeedback and performance (Landers, 1988; Petruzzello et al., 1991; Zaichkowsky and Fuchs, 1988). Studies on this issue have indicated that as a result of using biofeedback: (1) physiological stress levels decrease; (2) athletes' self-determined stress levels decrease; and (3) the two variables (physiological and self-determined stress levels) are not necessarily correlated (Tsukomoto, 1979).

BIOFEEDBACK AND MENTAL PREPARATION TECHNIQUES

Combining several procedures to examine the differential impact of each combination on the enhancement of sport and exercise performance has also been evident in research on biofeedback (e.g., Petruzzello et al., 1991). Biofeedback essentially involves a technological interface among external senses—the voluntary and autonomic branches of the central nervous system—in order to provide typically inaccessible information about biological states to the individual. It consists of training individuals to change various physiological indices (e.g., HR, muscle tension, brain activity) and to regulate physiological states with instrumentation, and then apply this ability to the situation without any instrumentation (whereas, ordinarily, the subjects would have been under exclusive autonomic control). Such autonomic control, however, may also be transferred to performance settings when biofeedback is absent (Basmajian, 1983; Green & Green, 1977).

According to Dishman (1987), biofeedback, in contrast to the other procedures investigated here, may be included in the group of somatic performance enhancement procedures, which minimize the role of cognitions in determining behavior while emphasizing objective situations and overt responses. Petruzzello et al. (1991) concluded that EMG biofeedback manipulations result in alterations of several physiological indices. They added that the exact nature of the relationship between these alterations and performance in various motor tasks is in need of further clarification, since biofeedback was not usually applied directly to athletic or motor tasks. Along these lines, in the Blumenstein, Bar-Eli, and Tenenbaum (1995) research, the mental techniques were specifically associated with the mental rehearsal/imagery of the performance task (100-m run) employed in the study and clearly demonstrated that when biofeedback is used as part of a larger intervention package (relaxation, imagery), its unique effect is an augmenting one. The same results were found in the research by Caird et al. (1999), in which HR biofeedback together with relaxation techniques improved running economy in a group of trained long-distance runners.

Several studies (Blais & Vallerand, 1986; Costa et al., 1984; Daniels & Landers, 1981) have demonstrated the positive effects of using biofeedback in conjunction with other psychological intervention techniques to control nonoptimal states that precede athletic competition (e.g., anxiety). In addition, Scartelli (1984) has demonstrated some positive effects of combining EMG biofeedback with sedative music. Goodspeed (1983) tested the efficacy of using electrodermal and temperature biofeedback as part of a comprehensive mental training program (relaxation, imagery, cognitive strategies) with gymnasts. Peper and Schmid (1983) studied the positive effects of temperature, EMG, and HR biofeedback with progressive relaxation, autogenic training, and imagery on enhancing athletic performance in members of the US rhythmic gymnastic team.

BIOFEEDBACK AND IMPROVED PERFORMANCE IN DIFFERENT SPORT DISCIPLINES

Research findings in the field of sport behavior and psychophysiology of exercise indicate that psychological stress during training and competition can be reduced by biofeedback training, and thus performance in different sport disciplines can be enhanced. In other studies, Dorsey (1976), Goodspeed (1983), Tsukomoto (1979), and Zaichkowsky (1983) found that a biofeedback training program (with EMG or GSR and temperature) helped gymnasts to control stress better and thus improve performance. The positive effects on members of the US rhythmic gymnastic team were demonstrated in a study by Peper and Schmid (1983). This 2-year biofeedback training program included EMG, GSR and temperature biofeedback training with progressive relaxation, autogenic training, and imagery, in addition to home practice. The gymnasts reported the program to be highly beneficial, enhancing their athletic performance, integrating mental skills into their workouts, and using relaxation to reenergize and control their arousal states.

In a series of field experiments, in which it was demonstrated that the Wingate five-step approach (Blumenstein et al., 1997b), a special mental program with biofeedback training (more details about this in the next chapter) may substantially enhance athletes' performance in applied settings. For example, Bar-Eli, Dreshman, Blumenstein, and Weinstein (2001) investigated the relationship between mental training with biofeedback (EMG, GSR, HR) and performance, using an adapted version (i.e., the first three steps) of the Wingate five-step approach as a mental preparation technique for enhancing the swimming performance among 11- to 14-year-old children swimmers. Participants were randomly assigned to one of the two conditions: (a) experimental—regular training plus three stages of the Wingate mental training program; and (b) control—regular training and relaxing activities. After a baseline measurement, participants were tested on evaluation scores and actual performance twice during a 14-week period. The results of this study indicated that the experimental group exhibited substantially greater increases (after 3.5 months) in training performance over time (although the control group also displayed some minor improvements), in terms of their results in real competitions as well as coaches' evaluations concerning their swimming technique.

In a more recent work, Shitrit (2001) (as part of his doctoral dissertation) used a similar research paradigm with 15- to 18-year-old athletes. In fact, Shitrit introduced replications in several respects, such as using three sport disciplines (swimming, basketball, and judo), two kinds of tasks (general and sport-specific), and two versions of the approach (the adapted one, with three steps, and the complete, five-step approach). In general, Shitrit (2001) found a similar pattern of results in comparison to the one revealed in the study by Bar-Eli et al. (2001), namely a quite consistent superiority of the experimental groups in all the field experiments conducted.

Several studies (Crews, Martin, Hart, & Piparo, 1991; Hatfield et al., 1984; Landers et al., 1991; Salazar, Landers, Petruzzello, Han, Crews, & Kubitz, 1990) have used left-hemisphere biofeedback training in precision sports like archery, shooting, and golf. These studies suggest that biofeedback training can improve athlete performance, but usually when the training is employed as a component of a larger "package" of mental skills interventions (for more details, see Petruzzello et al., 1991).

Table 3.1 presents a summary of the main approaches demonstrating the effect of biofeedback interventions with other mental techniques in different sports. These approaches demonstrate that if biofeedback can teach athletes to reduce muscle tension and anxiety and control arousal, then their performance should increase. According to Zaichkowsky and Fuchs (1986), competitive stress results in excessive arousal, which leads to disruption of thought, lack of concentration, confusion, and excessive body tension. These and other responses to stress result in the poor performance predicted by Yerkes and Dodson (1908). Biofeedback intervention should theoretically result in decreased muscle tension, autonomic responses, and self-report state anxiety. From this should follow increased athletic performance. At the same time, recent application of HR and EEG biofeedback to target sports has also been reported to be effective (Collins, 1995; Landers et al. 1991; Crews et al. 1991).

Table 3.1 Summary of main approaches demonstrating the biofeedback (BFB) interventions in different sports

Sport disciplines and author	BFB modalities	Mental techniques	Results
Gymnastics (Dorsey, 1976; Zaichkowsky, 1983; Goodspeed, 1983)	EMG, GSR, Temp.	Progressive relaxation, autogenic training, imagery	Improve motor control and performance
Rhythmic gymnastics (Peper & Schmid, 1983)	EMG, HR	Relaxation	Reduce muscle tension, improve self-report of performance
Shooting			
Rifle (Landers, 1985; Hatfield et al., 1984; 1987; Hatfield & Landers, 1987)	HR, respiration EEG	Progressive muscle relaxation	Help elite rifle shooters deal with performance anxiety
Pistol (Daniels & Landers, 1981)	EMG, GSR, respiration	Breathing techniques, imagery	
Archery (Salazar et al., 1990; Landers et al., 1991; Ren, 1995)	EEG, HR, EEG EMG		Improve athletic performance; Enhance postural consistence
Golf (Crews, 1991; Crews et al., 1991; Crews & Landers, 1993)	HR EEG EEG	Relaxation + imagery	Improve golf putting performance
Track & field			
Sprint—100m (Blumenstein, Bar-Eli, & Tenenbaum, 1995)	EMG	Autogenic training + imagery	Improve motor control and athletic performance
Long distance running (Caird et al., 1999)	HR	Relaxation	Improve running economy
Swimming (Blumenstein, Tenenbaum et al., 1995; Blumenstein, 1996; Bar-Eli, Dreshman, Blumenstein, Weinstein, 2001)	EMG, GSR, breathing	Relaxation + imagery	Decrease psychological prestart stress
	EMG, GSR, HR	Relaxation + imagery	Improve athletic performance
Synchronized swimming (Wentz & Strong, 1980)	EMG, Temp.	Relaxation + imagery	Better control of competition stress
Basketball and American football (De Witt, 1980)	EMG EMG + HR	Relaxation + imagery	Improve athletic performance

Table 3.1 (*continued*)

Sport disciplines and author	BFB modalities	Mental techniques	Results
Handball (Costa et al., 1984)	GSR	Relaxation training	Decrease precompetition anxiety
Karate (Collins et al., 1990)	EEG		Increase alpha band power, better attentional focus
Judo (Blumenstein et al., 1997b, Blumenstein, 1999)	EMG, GSR	Relaxation + imagery	Reduce competition stress, improve athletic performance
Canoeing, kayaking (Blumenstein & Bar-Eli, 1998)	EMG, GSR	Relaxation + imagery	Improve athletic performance
Winter sports (Kappers & Chapman, 1984)	Temp.	Autogenic training	Increase temperatures by relaxation

SUMMARY AND RECOMMENDATIONS FOR PRACTICE

In this chapter we attempted to review several studies and approaches in biofeedback application in sport and exercise.

1. Research findings in the field of sport behavior and psychophysiology of exercise indicated that psychological stress during training and performance can be reduced by biofeedback training and thus performance can be enhanced. However, biofeedback procedures employed for reducing anxiety and improving performance by reducing muscular tension, for strength training and induced muscle fatigue have been subjected to limited experimentation and thus need additional research to determine their efficacy.
2. Biofeedback training has some promising potential when it is used as part of a larger intervention package. Its only effect is an augmenting one (generally, biofeedback with relaxation and imagery techniques). However, this can explain why there has been a dearth of well-controlled studies of only biofeedback effects on performance in sport.
3. It cannot be concluded that biofeedback was the causal mechanism behind any performance changes. However, biofeedback research and practice offer promise for enhancing performance. Specifically, HR, EEG, and respiratory biofeedback training are related to performance in aiming tasks (archery, shooting, golf); temperature, EDA (GSR), and EMG biofeedback induce relaxation in sports where mental relaxation and concentration are crucial (e.g., gymnastics); EMG and GSR biofeedback training are used in combat sports (e.g., judo, wrestling); EMG, GSR, and breathing biofeedback training are used in swimming, biathlon, etc.

4. At the same time, details regarding biofeedback application methodology must be developed for sport (steps, load, session length, periodization, place in training). Moreover, sport practice requires more portable biofeedback devices for daily work in the field, in addition to friendly, understanding athletes and coaches who can make use of this information to improve the training process and the athletes' mental state.
5. In biofeedback applications two conditional approaches have been developed: the first traditional, which reflects the influence of the clinical direction of biofeedback application, and the second more sport-oriented, which is more connected to athletic performance and can be part of the sports training process. The first, typically traditional clinical biofeedback training in a laboratory setting, has the goal of reducing psychological stress (or reducing anxiety, muscular tension, etc.) and then improving performance. The second involves biofeedback training in a "step-by-step" regime from the lab to real training and competitions, utilizing testing and different simulative material. The goal of these two methods, which apparently complement each other, is to improve athletes' levels of self-regulation, optimize competitive behavior, and improve athletic performance.

REFERENCES

Andreassy, J. L. (2000). *Psychophysiology: Human behavior and physiological response* (4th ed). Hillsdale, NJ: Lawrence Erlbaum.

Anshel, M. (1995). Anxiety. In T. Morris & J. Summers (eds.), *Sport psychology, theory, applications and issues* (pp. 29–59). Brisbane: John Wiley & Sons.

Bar-Eli, M., Dreshman, R., Blumenstein, B., & Weinstein, Y. (2001). The effects of mental training with biofeedback on the performance of young swimmers. *Applied psychology: An International Review* (in press).

Basmajian, J. V. (ed.) (1983). *Biofeedback: Principles and practice for clinicians* (2nd ed). Baltimore: Williams & Wilkins.

Basmajian, J. V., & Wolf, S. L. (eds.) (1990). *Therapeutic exercise* (5th ed.). Baltimore: Williams & Wilkins.

Benson, H., Dryer, T., & Hartley, L. H. (1978). Decreased VO_2 consumption during exercise with elicitation of the relaxation response. *Journal of Human Stress*, **4**, 38–42.

Blais, M. R., & Vallerand, R. J. (1986). Multimodal effects of electro-myographic biofeedback: Looking at children's ability to control pre-competitive anxiety. *Journal of Sport Psychology*, **8**, 283–303.

Blumenstein, B. (1996). Psychological aspects of Olympic preparations. *Proceedings, 2nd Post-Olympic International Symposium; The Process of Training and Competition in View of the Atlanta '96 Games* (pp. 97–105). Wingate Institute, Israel.

Blumenstein, B. (1999). Mental training with biofeedback in combat sport. In V. Hosek, P. Tilinger, & L. Bilek (eds.), *Proceedings of the Xth European Congress of Sport Psychology, Part I* (pp. 119–121). Prague, Czech Republic: Charles University.

Blumenstein, B., & Bar-Eli, M. (1998). Self-regulation training with biofeedback training in elite canoers and kayakers. Special issue. In V. Issurin (ed.), *Science and practice of canoe/kayak high-performance training* (pp. 124–132). Elite Sport Department, Wingate Institute, Israel.

Blumenstein, B., & Bar-Eli, M. (2001). A five-step approach for biofeedback training in sport. *Sportwissenschaft*, 31(4), 412–424.

Blumenstein, B., Bar-Eli, M., & Tenenbaum, G. (1995). The augmenting role of biofeedback: Effects of autogenic, imagery, and music training on physiological indices and athletic performance. *Journal of Sports Sciences*, **13**, 343–354.

Blumenstein, B., Bar-Eli, M., & Tenenbaum, G. (1997a). Mental training in elite sport incorporating biofeedback. *Proceedings, IXth World Congress of Sport Psychology: Innovations in Sport Psychology: Linking Theory and Practice, Part I* (pp. 130–132). Wingate Institute, Israel.

Blumenstein, B., Bar-Eli, M., & Tenenbaum, G. (1997b). A five-step approach to mental training incorporating biofeedback. *The Sport Psychologist*, **11**, 440–453.

Blumenstein, B., Breslav, I., Bar-Eli, M., Tenenbaum, G., Weinstein, Y. (1995). Regulation of mental states and biofeedback techniques: Effects on breathing patterns. *Biofeedback and Self-Regulation*, **20**, 169–183.

Blumenstein, B., Tenenbaum, G., Bar-Eli, M., & Pie, J. (1995). Mental preparation techniques with elite athletes using computerized biofeedback and VCR. In W. Simpson, A. Le Unes, & J. Picou (eds.), *Applied research in coaching and athletics, annual* (pp. 1–16). Boston, MA: American Press.

Caird, S. J. A., McKenzie, A., & Sleivert, G. (1999). Biofeedback and relaxation techniques improve running economy in sub-elite long distance runners. *Medicine and Science in Sports and Exercise*, **31**, 717–722.

Collins, D. (1995). Psychophysiology and sport performance. In S. J. H. Biddle (ed.), *European perspectives on exercise and sport psychology* (pp. 154–178). Leeds, UK: Human Kinetics.

Collins, D., Powell, G., & Davies, I. (1990). An electroencephalographic study of hemispheric processing patterns during karate performance. *Journal of Sport and Exercise Psychology*, **12**, 223–234.

Collins, D. J., Powell, G. E., & Davies, I (1991). Cerebral activity prior to motion task performance: An electroencephalographic study. *Journal of Sport Sciences*, **9**, 313–324.

Costa, A., Bonaccorsi, N., & Scrimali, T. (1984). Biofeedback and control of anxiety preceeding athletic competition. *International Journal of Sport Psychology*, **15**, 98–109.

Crews, D. J. (1991). *The influence of attentive states on golf putting as indicated by cardial and electrocortical activity*. Eugene, OR: Microform.

Crews, D. J., & Landers, D. M. (1993). Electroencephalographic measures of attentional patterns prior to the golf putt. *Medicine and Science in Sports and Exercise*, **25**, 116–126.

Crews, D. J., Martin, J. J., Hart, E. A., & Piparo, A. J. (1991). The effectiveness of EEG biofeedback, relaxation and imagery training on golf putting performance. Paper presented at the North American Society for the Psychology of Sport and Physical Activity (NASPSPA) Annual Conference, Asilomar, California.

Croce, R. V. (1986). The effects of EMG biofeedback on strength acquisition. *Biofeedback Self-Regulation*, **11**, 299–310.

Daniels, R., & Landers, D. M. (1981). Biofeedback and shooting performance: A test of disregulation and systems theory. *Journal of Sport Psychology*, **3**, 271–282.

Davis, H. (1991). Passive recovery and optimal arousal in ice hockey. *Perceptual and Motor Skills*, **72**, 1–2.

De Pascalis, V., Anello, A., & Venturini, R. (1986). Changes in heart rate during feedback control of respiration. *Perceptual and Motor Skills*, **63**, 87–96.

De Witt, D. J. (1980). Cognitive and biofeedback training for stress reduction with university athletes. *Journal of Sport Psychology*, **2**, 288–294.

Dishman, R. K. (1987). Psychological aids to performance. In R. H. Strauss (ed.), *Drugs and performance in sports* (pp. 121–146). Philadelphia, PA: Saunders.

Dorsey, J. A. (1976). The effects of biofeedback assisted desensitization training on state anxiety and performance of college age gymnasts. Unpublished doctoral dissertation, Boston University.

Edwards, R. G., & Lippold, O. C. (1956). The relationship between force and integrated electrical activity in fatigued muscle. *Journal of Physiology*, **132**, 677.

French, S. N. (1978). Electromyographic feedback for tension control during five motor skill acquisitions. *Perceptual Motor Skills*, **47**, 883–889.

Freedman, R. (1991). Physiological mechanisms of temperature biofeedback. *Biofeedback and Self-Regulation*, **16**, 95–115.

Goodspeed, G. A. (1983). The effects of comprehensive self-regulation training on state anxiety and performance of female gymnasts. Unpublished doctoral dissertation, Boston University.

Green, E., & Green, A. (1977). *Beyond biofeedback.* New York: Delacorte.

Griffiths, J. J., Steel, D. H., Vaccaro, P., & Karpman, M. B. (1981). The effects of relaxation techniques on anxiety and underwater performance. *International Journal of Soprt Psychology*, **12**, 176–182.

Hatch, J., Borchberding, S., & Norris, I. (1990). Cardiopulmonary adjustments during operant heart rate control. *Psychophysiology*, **27**, 611–618.

Hatfield, B. D., & Landers, D. M. (1987). Psychophysiology in exercise and sport research: An overview. *Exercise and Sport Science Reviews*, **15**, 351–388.

Hatfield, B. D., Landers, D. M., & Ray, W. J. (1984). Cognitive processes during self-paced motor performance: An electroencephalographic study of elite rifle shooters. *Journal of Sport Psychology*, **6**, 42–59.

Hatfield, B. D., Landers, D. M., & Ray, W. J. (1987). Cardiovascular – CNS interactions during a self-paced, intentional attentive state: Elite marksmanship performance. *Psychophysiology*, **24**, 542–549.

Jacobson, E. (1938). *Progressive relaxation*. Chicago: University of Chicago Press.

Kamimura, M., & Kodama, M. (1995). The effect of the peripheral skin temperature biofeedback training on stage fright. In F. H. Fu & M. L. Ng (eds.), *Sport psychology: Perspectives and practices toward the 21*st *century* (pp. 347–35). Hong Kong: Hong Kong Baptist University.

Kappers, B. M., & Chapman, S. J. (1984). The effect of indoor versus outdoor thermal biofeedback training in cold weather sports. *Journal of Sport psychology*, **6**, 305–311.

Kondo, C. V., Canter, J. A., & Bean, J. H. (1977). Intersession interval and reductions in frontalis EMG during biofeedback training. *Psychophysiology*, **1**, 15–17.

Krueger, K. M., Ruehl, M., Scheel, D., & Franz, U. (1988). Die Anwendbarkeit von EMG Biofeedback zur Optimierung sportlicher Techniken im motorischen Lernprozess von Ausdauersportarten am Beispiel des Kanurennsports. *Theorie und Praxis Leistungssport (Leipzig)*, **26**, 128–142.

Landers, D. M. (1985). Psychophysiological assessment and biofeedback. In J. Sandweiss & S. Wolf (eds.), *Biofeedback and sport science* (pp. 63–105). New York: Plenum.

Landers, D. M. (1988). Improving motor skills. In D. Druckman & J. A. Swets (eds.). *Enhancing human performance* (pp. 61–101). Washington, DC: National Academy Press.

Landers, D. M., Petruzzello, S. J., Salazar, W., Crews, D. L., Kubitz, K. A., Gannon, T. L., & Han, M. (1991). The influence of electrocortical biofeedback on performance in pre-elite archers. *Medicine and Science in Sport and Exercise*, **23**, 123–129.

Lloyd, A. J. (1972). Auditory EMG feedback during sustained submaximum isometric contractions. *Research Quarterly*, **43**, 39–46.

Lucca, J. A., & Recchiuti (1983). Effect of electromyographic biofeedback on an isometric strengthening program. *Physical Therapy*, **63**, 200–203.

Mador, M. J., & Tobin, M. J. (1991). Effect of alteration in mental activity on the breathing pattern in healthy subjects. *American Review of Respiratory Diseases*, **144**, 481–487.

Martens, A. (1977). *Sport competition anxiety test.* Champaign, IL: Human Kinetics.

McGlynn, G. H., Laughlin, N. T., & Filios, S. P. (1979). The effect of electromyographic feedback and static stretching on artificially induced muscle soreness. *American Journal of Physical Medicine*, **58**, 139–148.

Middaugh, S. J., Miller, M. C., Foster, G., Ferdon, M. B. (1982). Electromyographic feedback: Effects of voluntary muscle contractions in normal subjects. *Archives of Physical and Medical Rehabilitation*, **63**, 254–260.

Moran, A. P. (1996). The psychology of concentration in sport performers: A cognitive analysis. UK: Psychology Press – an imprint of Erlbaum (UK), Taylor & Francis, Ltd.

Nielsen, D. H., & Holmes, D. S. (1980). Effectiveness of EMG biofeedback training for controlling arousal in subsequent stressful situations. *Biofeedback and Self-Regulation*, **5**, 235–245.

Pack, D., & McCool, F. D. (1992). Breathing pattern during varied activities. *Journal of Applied Physiology*, **73**, 887–893.

Peek, C. J. (1987). A primer of biofeedback instrumentation. In M. S. Schwartz (ed.), *Biofeedback: A practitioner's guide* (pp. 73–127). New York: The Guilford Press.

Peper, E., & Schmid, A. (1983). The use of electrodermal biofeedback for peak performance training. *Somatics*, **4**, 16–18.

Peper, E., & Tibbetts, V. (1992). Fifteen month follow-up with asthmatics utilizing EMG/incentive inspirometer feedback. *Biofeedback and Self-Regulation*, **17**, 143–151.

Perski, A., Tzankoff, S. P., & Engel, B. T. (1985). Central control of cardiovascular adjustment to exercise. *Journal of Applied Physiology*, **58**, 431–435.

Petruzzello, S. J., Landers, D. M., & Salazar, W. (1991). Biofeedback and sport/exercise performance: Applications and limitations. *Behavior Therapy*, **22**, 379–392.

Ren W.-D. (1995). A study of EMG biofeedback for improving archery postural consistency. In F. H. Fu & M. L. Ng (eds.), *Sport psychology: Perspectives and practices toward the 21st century* (pp. 261–265). Hong Kong Baptist University, Hong Kong.

Sabourin, M., & Rioux, S. (1979). Effects of active and passive EMG biofeedback training on performance of motor and cognitive tasks. *Perceptual and Motor Skills*, **49**, 831–835.

Salazar, W., Landers, D., Petruzzello, S., Han, M., Crews, D., & Kubitz, K. (1990). Hemispheric asymmetry, cardiac response and performance in elite archers. *Research Quarterly for Exercise and Sport*, **61**, 351–359.

Sandweiss, J. H. (1985). Biofeedback and sport sciences. In J. Sandweiss & S. Wolf (eds.), *Biofeedback and sport sciences* (pp. 5–13). New York: Plenum.

Sandweiss, J. H., & Wolf, S. (eds.). (1985). *Biofeedback and sport sciences.* New York: Plenum.

Scartelli, J. P. (1984). The effect of EMG biofeedback and sedative music, EMG biofeedback only, and sedative music only on frontalis muscle relaxation ability. *Journal of Music Therapy*, **21**, 67–78.

Schwartz, M. S. (1987). *Biofeedback: A practitioner's guide.* New York: The Guilford Press.

Shellenberger, R., & Green, J. A. (1986). *From the ghost in the box to successful biofeedback training.* Greeley, CO: Health Psychology Publications.

Shitrit, D. (2001). *The influence of mental training with biofeedback on the motor performance of teenagers engaging in sport.* Unpublished doctoral dissertation, submitted to the Department of Physical Education, Anglia Polytechnic University, Essex, UK.

Standards and guidelines for biofeedback applications in psychophysiological self-regulation (1992). Wheat Ridge, CO: Association for Applied Psychophysiology and Biofeedback.

Teague, M. A. (1976). A combined systematic desensitization and electromyograph biofeedback technique for controlling state anxiety and improving motor skill performance. Unpublished Ph.D. Dissertation, University of Northern Colorado, Greeley, Colorado.

Tsukomoto, S. (1979). The effects of EMG biofeedback assisted relaxation on sport competition anxiety. Unpublished master's thesis. University of Western Ontario, London, Ontario.

Walter, W. G. (1963). *The living brain.* New York: W. W. Norton

Weinberg, R. S., & Hunt, V. V. (1976). The interrelationships between anxiety, motor performance and electromyography. *Journal of Motor Behavior*, **9**, 219–224.

Wenz, B. J., & Strong, D. J. (1980). An application of biofeedback and self-regulation procedures with superior athletes. In R. W. Suinn (ed.), *Psychology in sports: Methods and applications* (pp. 328–333). Minneapolis: Burgess.

Yerkes, R. M., Dodson, J. O. (1908). The relation of strength of stimulus to rapidity of habit formation. *Journal of Comparative Neurology and Psychology*, **18**, 459–482.

Zaichkowsky, L. D. (1983). The use of biofeedback for self-regulation of performance states. In L. E. Unestahl (ed.), *The mental aspects of gymnastics* (pp. 95–105). Örebro, Sweden: Veje.

Zaichkowsky, L. D., Dorsey, J. A., & Mulholland, T. B. (1979). The effects of biofeedback assisted systematic desensitization in the control of anxiety and performance. In M. Vanek (ed.), *IV Svetovy Kongress, ISSP* (pp. 809–812). Prague: Olympia.

Zaichkowsky, L. D., & Fuchs, C. Z. (1986). Biofeedback: The psychophysiology of motor control and human performance. In L. Zaichkowsky & C. Fuchs (eds.), *The psychology of motor behavior: Development, control, learning and performance* (pp. 159–173). Ithaca, NY: Mouvement.

Zaichkowsky, L. D., & Fuchs, C. Z. (1988). Biofeedback applications in exercise and athletic performance. In K. B. Pandolf (ed.), *Exercise and sports sciences reviews* (pp. 381–421). New York: Macmillan.

Zaichkowsky, L. D., & Takenaka, K. (1993). Optimizing arousal level. In R. N. Singer, M. Murphey, & L. K. Takenaka (eds.), *Handbook of research on sport psychology* (pp. 511–527). New York: Macmillan.

CHAPTER 4

Biofeedback Training in Sport

Boris Blumenstein, Michael Bar-Eli, and Dave Collins

In Chapter 3 we discussed the current state in applied biofeedback research in the different directions, and demonstrated the positive effects of using biofeedback in conjunction with other psychological interventions. In Chapter 4, we will describe two examples of biofeedback training programs in different sports. The first one is a training program with several biofeedback modalities originally presented by Blumenstein, Bar-Eli, and Tenenbaum (1997) entitled "The Wingate five-step approach," and the second a training program with EEG biofeedback presented by Collins.

THE WINGATE FIVE-STEP APPROACH

The Wingate five-step approach for mental training incorporating biofeedback with VCR consists of five stages, with flexible time-session units that can be individualized. These are (1) introduction (i.e., learning various self-regulation techniques), (2) identification (i.e., identifying and strengthening the most efficient biofeedback response modality), (3) simulation (i.e., biofeedback training with simulated competitive stress), (4) transformation (i.e., proceeding preparation from laboratory to field), and (5) realization (i.e., obtaining optimal regulation in competition). Figure 4.1 gives a schematic representation of the Wingate five-step approach to mental preparation with biofeedback. In the following, these steps and training sessions will be presented briefly (for more detail, see Blumenstein et al., 1997).

The first step, the Introduction, takes place in a laboratory setting, where the athlete is introduced to the various pieces of psychophysiological equipment, including the computerized biofeedback and VCR equipment. This step, which takes about 10–15 sessions, 2–3 times a week, with each session lasting about 55–60 min, consists of teaching the athlete to regulate his or her mental state through observing the psychophysiological responses on the screen. The athlete begins with the frontalis

Brain and Body in Sport and Exercise: Biofeedback Applications in Performance Enhancement.
Edited by Boris Blumenstein, Michael Bar-Eli, and Gershon Tenenbaum.

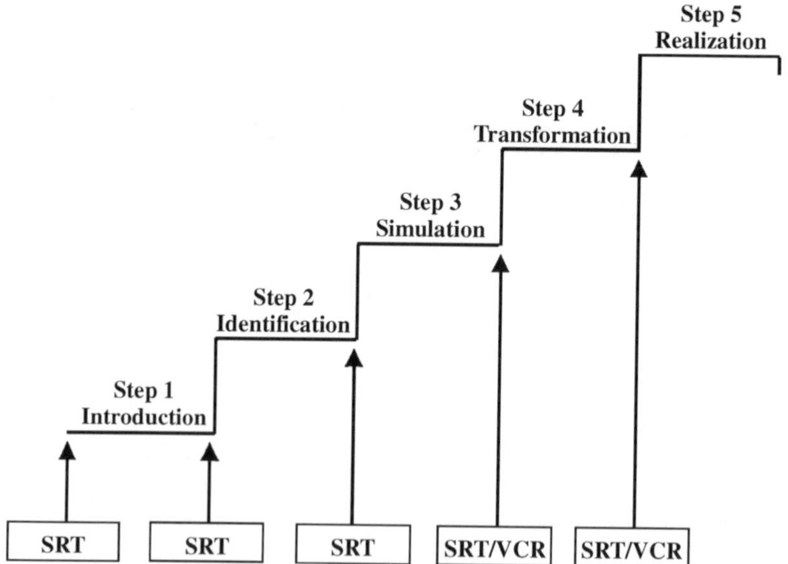

Figure 4.1 The five-step approach to mental preparation with biofeedback

EMG feedback with surface electrodes placed on the frontalis muscle in accordance with Kondo, Canter, and Bean (1977). Later in this step (and in all the following steps), the athlete also uses other biofeedback modalities, such as galvanic skin response (GSR) and heart rate (HR) or breathing.

Table 4.1 gives an example of a training plan for the few last sessions of step 1. It should be noted that this plan is flexible so that the specific performance requirements of each athlete, who has to fulfill a particular task in a given environment, can be met. In the last sessions it is very important for the athlete to feel his or her muscles, thoughts, and breathing changes, in order to experience their consequent influence on biofeedback modalities. For example, the athlete's concentration on relaxing nature pictures is reflected through consequent physiological relaxation (i.e., HR, GSR, and EMG changes).

The goal of this entire introductory learning phase is to achieve a stable process in which the athlete relaxes for about 2–3 min, maintains a deep relaxation for about 5–10 min, and then rehearses excitation for about 2–3 min (see Blumenstein, Tenenbaum, Bar-Eli, & Pie, 1995). After terminating the learning phase, the athlete undergoes a self-regulation test (SRT) to indicate his or her psychoregulative level and to observe the specific modalities pertaining to his or her individual responses. Table 4.2 shows schematically the nature and the direction of psychophysiological changes in the SRT.

SRT is used to examine the athlete's baseline self-regulation level before the mental training program is applied, and later during the various steps of the program.

Table 4.1 An example of the biofeedback training session at step 1. Lesson duration: 55–60 min

Beginning	Basic work	Final work
Warm-up with relaxation–excitation muscle exercises (hands, feet, hands and feet)—2–3 × 5–7 min	Audio EMG_{BFB}—muscle relaxation–excitation with EMG feedback (EMG from baseline to 0.8–1.0 μV and from 0.8–1.0 μV to 2.2–2.4 μV)—2 × 5 min	Relaxation with audio cassette recorded (relaxation music)—10 min
	Audiovisual GSR_{BFB}—muscle relaxation–excitation exercises with GSR feedback—2 × 5–10 min	
	Concentration exercises with GSR control—2 × 5 min	
	Audio HR_{BFB}—muscle relaxation–excitation exercises with HR feedback, discussion of connection between breathing pattern and HR feedback	

BFB, biofeedback.

Essentially, the SRT consists of three elements: rest, tension, and warmth. They were derived and modified from the autogenic training technique suggested by Schultz (1970). After recording the athlete's psychophysiological baseline (HR, GSR, EMG), the athlete is asked to imagine him- or herself in the laboratory setting, in resting, tense, and warm states, consecutively. However, to orient the athlete to competition, the athlete is also asked to imagine him- or herself in a fourth state, namely competition. Towards the end of each of these imagery phases, lasting about 2 min each, the athlete's psychophysiological responses (HR, GSR, EMG) are recorded, to indicate the type of alteration in each response modality as well as its relative intensity. It should be noted that for diagnostic purposes, the changes recorded following the phase of competition imagery are of particular significance. The arrows in Table 4.2 represent the expected direction of positive change on each psychophysiological modality in

Table 4.2 Direction of psychophysiological changes from baseline in self-regulation test (SRT)

	Physiological responses		
	HR	GSR	EMG
Rest	↓	↑	↓
Tension	↑	↓	↑
Warmth	↓	↑	↓
Competition	↑	↓	↑

each phase when imagery is indeed effective (+). The sport psychologist notes the direction and intensity of the observed changes. However, in order to establish the unique pattern tht characterizes each and every athlete, the relations between the various psychophysiological indices (with regard to direction and intensity), as well as the relations within and between the imagery phases, should be followed. After eight years' experience and application of our program in different sports, we can conclude that our best elite athletes achieved in SRT:

11–12+ (positive changes in HR, GSR, EMG channels)—high self-regulation abili- ties (maximum possible result is 12+)
8–10+ (positive changes in HR, GSR, EMG channels)—average self-regulation abilities
6–7+ (positive changes in HR, GSR, EMG channels)—low self-regulation abilities

For self-regulation, in the beginning elite athletes used the HR and EMG channels better than the GSR channel.

The central purpose of step 2, Identification, (which includes about 15 sessions) is to identify and strengthen the athlete's most efficient response modality on the biofeedback. This modality is modified by the individual's specific personal psychophysiologic characteristics, and by the characteristics of the sport discipline in which the athlete competes. Moreover, different sports require different response modalities. For example, in judo or wrestling, in which performance involves high levels of tactile and proprioceptive sensitivity and intense emotional involvement, EMG and GSR seem to be the most efficient modalities to measure. In contrast, rifle shooting demands a shooter's postural, breathing, and muscle stability, and therefore EEG is more suitable (Landers, Petruzzello, Salazar, Crews, Kubitz, Gannon, & Han, 1991). Finally, HR and breathing frequency (f_b) are more useful for long-distance running or swimming, which require mainly cardiopulmonary and cardiomuscular endurance.

In line with these considerations, the central purpose of step 2 is to identify the athlete's most efficient biofeedback modality, in terms of his or her personal characteristics and the demands of the sport discipline in which he or she is active.

In Table 4.3, an example of step 2 is presented. This example is taken from the applied work conducted with one of Israel's and the world's best judokas (who won, among others, the silver medal in the 1995 World Championship and the bronze medal in the 1992 Olympics).

In this step, relaxation–excitation speed and relaxation–excitation level are highly important—for example, to achieve EMG relaxation within the limits 0.8–1.0 μV during 1–3 min, or excitation with imagery within the limits 1.8–2.2 μV during 1 min. The athlete must be able to perform (in the laboratory setting) the required relaxation–excitation cycles—quickly, accurately, and reliably.

To strengthen the preferred response modality, the athlete repeats the entire procedure learned in step 1 using only this modality for the next ten sessions. Again, imagery is practiced with "soft eyes," to enable the athlete to attend to the biofeedback information presented on the computer screen. Auditory feedback is also provided in

Table 4.3 An example of the biofeedback training session at step 2 (judo). Lesson duration: 50–60 min

Beginning	Basic work	Final work
Warm-up with relaxation–excitation muscle exercises (hands, feet, hands and feet)—2–3 × 5–7 min	EMG_{BFB} training—relaxation with EMG feedback (EMG from baseline to 1.0–1.4 μV—in audio and visual versions)—3–4 × 5 min. Control and analysis of other BFB channels (HR, GSR)	Relaxation with GSR_{BFB} and special relaxation music without words—5–10 min
	EMG_{BFB} training (EMG from baseline to 0.8–1.4 μV) during definite time periods: 1, 3, 5, 7 min	
	EMG_{BFB} training—relaxation + imagery (IM)—excitation (competition situation—EMG in limits 2.2–3.2 μV)—10–15 min	

this process. Following step 2, the SRT is again conducted, to identify the harmonic response level of the athlete in several modalities.

In the third step, Simulation, the athlete mentally practices in the natural environment for about 15 sessions, 2–3 times a week, with each session lasting about 50–60 min. Specifically, at the beginning of this phase (sessions 1–3), video scenes from competitive situations in which the athlete competed are presented on the VCR screen. While watching the scenes, a mental cycle of relaxation–excitation states is rehearsed. These states are geared to the particular competition needs at each moment of competition, as well as the athlete's personal characteristics. For example, in combat sports (e.g., judo, fencing, taekwondo, wrestling, or boxing), there are several breaks between the rounds. During these breaks, it is advisable for the athlete to be engaged in some self-regulatory activity that is focused mainly on the transition from relaxation to excitation, in order to psych up for the next round. In contrast, following the entire match, a transition from excitation to relaxation is needed. This enables the athlete to learn his or her moves and prepare for the next match. This activity may last for 3–15 min, depending on the athlete's specific requirements. To optimally use the available options, the sport psychologist should acquire extensive knowledge about both the athlete and the particular sport.

The athlete practices the shifts from one mental state to another by observing 5–10 scenes, lasting for about 10–30 s each. The order of the scenes may be of importance, depending, among other things, on the athlete's preferences. From sessions 4 to 15, the VCR apparatus is used to simulate competitive stress presented to the athlete. The main principle guiding the use of VCR in this step is a gradual elevation of the simulated stress.

Recently, however, we started to simultaneously use a video camera as well, in order to film the athletes' facial expressions during the step 3 training (Figure 4.2).

Table 4.4 An example of the biofeedback training session at step 3 (wrestling). Lesson duration: 55–65 min

Beginning	Basic work	Final work
BFB warm-up with relaxation–excitation muscle exercises 5, 3, 1 min with different BFB channels (HR, GSR, EMG)—10–15 min	VCR scenes (competition fragments) and 1, 3, 5 min relaxation version with EMG–GSR_{BFB} VCR scenes with competitive fragments and 1 min relaxation with GSR_{BFB}; IM competition fragments and 1 min relaxation—2–3 times VCR scenes with concrete competitive fights and 1–2 min relaxation with EMG_{BFB}; 3–5 min observation of own competition preparation and 1–2 min competition match, as well as IM accompanied by GSR_{BFB}. All procedures are recorded by the sport psychologist using a video camera; then the videotaped athletes' behavioral reactions, then IM and behavioral responses are discussed.	Relaxation with GSR_{BFB}, accompanied by specially prepared relaxing music—5 min

IM, imagery.

The aim of this "double-feedback" procedure is to facilitate facial self-regulation. This is crucial not only to enable the athlete to better control his or her own emotional side through regulation of facial expression during competition, but also for competitive purposes, e.g., to deceive his or her rival.

Table 4.4 presents an example of the last sessions of step 3. This example is taken from the applied work conducted with one of Israel's and the world's best wrestlers

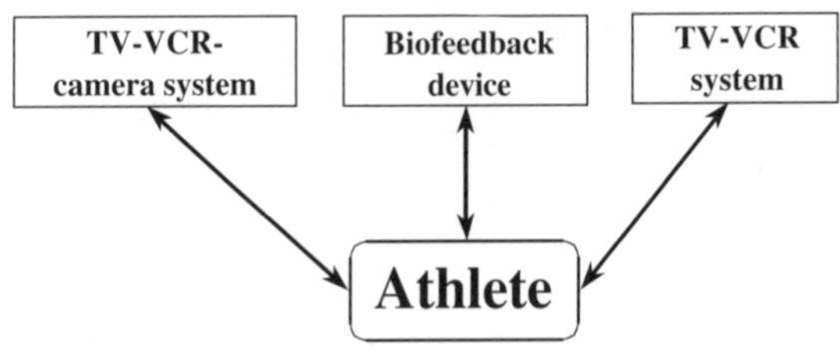

Figure 4.2 Elements of the biofeedback and VCR system ("double" biofeedback version)

(second in the European Championship in 1994 and in the World Championship in 1995, fifth in the Olympic Games in 1996, and sixth in the Olympic Games in 2000).

At the end of step 3, the athlete feels mentally prepared and self-confident. Accordingly, his or her observed biofeedback reactions are quick and accurate.

After completing step 3, the athlete is re-tested using the SRT procedure. However, in contrast to the previous steps, the SRT procedure is now accompanied by VCR presentations. The athlete's psychophysiological indices during the rest, tension, warmth, and competition phases (see Table 4.2) are recorded in response to a familiar videotaped presentation of the athlete in an important competition. This helps to identify the level of stability with which the athlete is able to regulate his or her arousal.

In the fourth phase, Transformation, which includes about 15 sessions, the athlete mentally prepares for a specific upcoming competition. The material learned and rehearsed by the athlete in steps 1–3 is transferred into actual training settings, in contrast to the laboratory setting in which the previous steps were conducted.

For example, after completing the warm-up, the athlete is instructed to conduct a 1-min mental relaxation using central elements of autogenic training (usually through key words used as cues), while being attached to the portable biofeedback apparatus. Then, for 2 min he or she generates vivid images of the next specific moves to be performed in the practice session (e.g., performing a particular technical element) in order to reach the appropriate excitatory state needed for this particular move.

During practice, the athlete may use some elements from the procedure to prevent an upcoming psychological crisis state. For example, during long-distance running, the athlete can concentrate on a particular tensed or exhausted body part, to relax and refresh this body part through the mental technique previously learned. Towards later training sessions in this stage, videotape presentations of the athlete's upcoming competitor(s) are introduced. This is accompanied by excitatory and energizing imagery that the athlete uses for mental preparatory purposes. In addition, the mental procedure (including biofeedback and VCR) is rehearsed for 3–5 min to facilitate recovery between different practice units and/or following the complete practice. Specifically, immediately after the practice, the athlete is exposed to VCR films that include pastoral visual scenes accompanied by calm and relaxing music.

Table 4.5 presents an example of step 4. This example is taken from a 17-year-old female taekwondoist, who in 1998 represented Israel in the Junior World Championship and won the silver medal.

Thus, the main purpose of step 4 is to enable the athlete to enter real future competitions with an improved self-regulation ability.

After completing step 4, the athlete undergoes the SRT accompanied by the VCR. This is done in order to estimate his or her stability and readiness in applying the entire technique for self-regulation purposes in real-life settings.

In the fifth step, Realization, the athlete applies the previously acquired mental techniques during competition. Essentially, the application is very similar to that practiced in the training (see step 4), but at this stage it is applied during the competition itself. The athlete begins by applying the procedure in relatively less important competitions. Biofeedback is used in different competitive settings. For example, in

Table 4.5 An example of the biofeedback training session at step 4 (taekwondo). Lesson duration: according to training time

Beginning	Basic work	Final work
In the end of training warm-up—relaxation–excitation exercises with portable EMG_{BFB}—1–3 min	Relaxation with portable EMG or GSR_{BFB} between training matches—2–3 × 1 min	Relaxation at the end of training with portable EMG–GSR_{BFB}—5–10 min
	Excitation and concentration with portable GSR_{BFB} between training matches—2–3 × 1 min	
	Relaxation–excitation with IM, includes tactical preparation elements with portable GSR_{BFB}—1–2 × 3 min	

sailing and windsurfing it is used 20–25 min before the start on board (relaxation–excitation pattern with a following start imagery, 3–5 min), between competition races (relaxation–excitation pattern, 5–10 min). In judo, wrestling, and taekwondo, it is used, for example, 20–25 min before the start (relaxation–excitation pattern with imagery of tactical plan for upcoming match as well as between matches; relaxation with analysis of past matches, 5–10 min, and excitation before next match, 1–3 min). The realization step of the program lasts for about ten sessions. During these sessions the level of competition used in conjunction with the mental training procedure is gradually increased, until the athlete is ready for important competitions. This ensures that the athlete gradually learns to cope with increasingly difficult situations and to become less crisis-vulnerable (Bar-Eli, Tenenbaum, & Elbaz, 1989).

The five-step approach was successfully applied by different Israeli elite athletes in various top-level events (two Olympic Games and four European and three World championships in different sports). In the following we will provide several examples of using this approach in various sport disciplines with elite athletes.

APPLICATION OF THE WINGATE FIVE-STEP APPROACH TO DIFFERENT SPORT DISCIPLINES

The Wingate five-step approach was built in line with an important principle, from the general to the specific (Bompa, 1994), and thus it is highly flexible in its ability to adapt to match specific needs of individual athletes fulfilling particular discipline-specific tasks within given environments. The specific characteristics of various sport disciplines should be taken into consideration, particularly in the second (specificity) step of the entire program. In sports that require speed and power (such as sprinting, jumping, and weight-lifting), focusing and concentration are of primary importance. In aerobic sports (such as long-distance running and swimming), perception of rhythm, accuracy of movement, and pain tolerance are highly necessary. In ball games and combat sports (such as judo, boxing, wrestling, taekwondo, and fencing), cognitive capabilities (e.g., attention and anticipation) are required. Accordingly, mental preparation techniques should fit into the specific requirements of each sport discipline, as was noted as early as 1970 in the classic work by Vanek and Cratty (1970).

The mental procedure introduced here suggests an efficient method of learning to control one's emotions and shift arousal states in accordance with the specific course of the competition. The frequency with which such shifts of mental states are required for performance maximization is dependent upon the unique determinants of each sport discipline.

In the following, we will discuss in more detail the biofeedback training (five-step approach) in several sport disciplines, which has been applied in Israel for mental preparation in elite sport, such as judo, swimming, canoeing, and kayaking (for more practical details, see Blumenstein, 1999; Blumenstein & Bar-Eli, 1998, 2001).

Sailing and Windsurfing

In sailing and windsurfing, competitive performance not only involves high endurance and speed, but it is also regulated by the opponents and meteorological conditions from the start and during the entire race or regatta. Often waiting for suitable weather, decision-making speed, and cognitive processes in critical situations during a regatta or race impact on athletes' performance. In addition, sailors and windsurfers are require to conduct numerous starts with in relatively short time periods (i.e., 11 starts in 6 competitive days in the Sydney 2000 Olympic Games in the 470 class). Accordingly, most coaches and sailors and windsurfers would agree that mental control, mental toughness, and self-regulation are necessary for successful performance.

Table 4.6 outlines the general principles of a mental training program developed for and applied to elite Israeli sailors/windsurfers in the 470 and Mistral classes. This program is based on the original five-step approach (see Blumenstein et al., 1997). In Table 4.7, an example of an appropriate general precompetition weekly mental training program applied to elite Israeli athletes is presented, based on steps 4 and 5 of the entire program. It should be noted that on the basis of such general principles, specific programs for shorter time periods (e.g., month, week, or day) can be derived.

In practice, mental preparation is integrated into athletes' regular training (e.g., conditioning or technical and tactical training in line with Bompa's 1994 recommendations). In order to achieve maximum efficiency, the sport psychologist is advised to cooperate closely with coach and athletes over time, and eventually become an integral part of the coaching team, to improve mutual cooperation (see Bar-Eli & Tenenbaum, 1989).

Table 4.6 Principles of a mental training program for sailing/windsurfing athletes

	Mode and length of treatment (sessions × time)	Content
Step 1: Introduction	Group 5–8 × 30 min Individual 5–8 × 25 min	Meetings and workshops with coaches and athletes; introduction of psychological techniques (AT, muscle relaxation, self-talk, BFB); application of relaxation games and self-regulation test
Step 2*: Identification	Individual—group 10–15 × 30 min	BFB training with HR, GSR, and EMG modalities; self-regulation test
Step 3*: Simulation	Individual—group 20–25 × 3 min	BFB training with imagery on beach and in boat (planning competition situations; e.g., pre-start, start, etc.), self-regulation test
	Individual 10–15 × 30 min	Concentration training on beach and in boat (self-talk, imagery, breathing, BFB, muscle relaxation)
Step 4: Transformation	During training, between races 20–25 × 4–5 min	Mental training in boat (relaxation and recovery in boat with portable GSR_{BFB}), self-regulation test
	20–25 × 1–2 min	Brief relaxation
Step 5: Realization	During or between competitions 10–15 × 10–15 min	Pre-start competition support; planning competition versions (on shore); recovery between races.

AT, autogenic training.
* Homework for steps 2–3: mental recovery with music; special relaxation program with portable GSR_{BFB}; 5–10 × 15–20 min.
Daily relaxation practice with portable GSR_{BFB}; extended relaxation, 2–3 × 15 min; brief relaxation, 4–5 × 5 min; brief relaxation, 6–8 × 1 min.

Combat Sports

Competitions in elite combat sports require high levels of attention and concentration, will power, and self-control. Combat situations in judo, taekwondo, boxing, fencing, and wrestling may change within extremely short periods of time (e.g., one-tenth of a second); accordingly, emotional states during combat matches are subject to extreme fluctuations. It is often difficult for the competing athlete to attack and to defend at the same time, to hide his/her feelings and to discover those of the opponent, to keep a "poker face" when nerves are extremely tense, to make decisions under time pressure, to be flexible in tactical movements, and, last but not least, to persistently strive for the assigned goals. Psychological preparation for combat sports should therefore be derived from these requirements, in line with the psychological profile not only of elite wrestlers (Eklund, Gould, & Jackson, 1993; Highlen & Bennett, 1979), but also of combat sports in general (Nowicki, 1989).

Table 4.7 General pre-competition weekly mental training program (sailing)

Sunday	Monday	Tuesday	Wednesday	Thursday (competition day)	Friday (competition day)
Concentration exercises on beach—5 min Muscle relaxation in boat—4–6 × 1 min Brief relaxation after training with portable GSR_{BFB}—5 min	Concentration exercise on beach—5 min Muscle relaxation in boat—5–6 × 1 min Brief relaxation after training with portable GSR_{BFB}—5 min	Homework with portable GSR_{BFB}—brief relaxation–excitation cycles, 2–3 × 1–3 min	Imagery on shore: (technical elements) and start information exchange and communication in boat before and during start—2 × 3 min Mental recovery after training 15–20 min with portable GSR_{BFB}	20–25 min before start: Concentration exercises in boat—2–3 min Imagery before start—2–3 × 1–3 min Relaxation after race with portable GSR_{BFB}—1–5 min	20–25 min before start: Concentration exercises in boat—2–3 min Imagery before start—2–3 × 1–3 min Relaxation after race with portable GSR_{BFB}—1–5 min

Table 4.8 Principles of a mental training program for combat sport athletes (judo, wrestling, taekwondo)

Steps	Mode and length of treatment (sessions × time)	Content
Step 1*: Introduction	Group 5–6 × 30 min	Meetings and workshops with coaches and athletes; special psychophysiological diagnosis (self-regulation test, reaction time, special feeling: muscle, time reproduction); goal setting; introductions of mental techniques:
	Individual 10–15 × 30–45 min	AT, muscle relaxation, imagery and concentration training exercise, BFB training
Step 2*: Identification	Individual 10–15 × 30 min	BFB training with GSR and EMG modalities (planning recovery between fights), self-regulation test
Step 3*: Simulation	Individual 20–30 × 20 min	BFB training with AT and imagery and VCR system (planning competition situations: e.g., pre-start mental preparation), tactical–technical preparation before fights).
	15–20 × 5–10 min	BFB training with EMG, GSR modalities after VCR demonstration and during VCR interventions. Self-regulation test
Step 4: Transformation	Individual—group 20–30 × 1–3 min 20–30 × 3–5 min 10–15 × 10–15 min	Mental practice in training hall (between and after training fights): brief relaxation–excitation in pre-start preparation, recovery between fights, relaxation after training. Self-regulation test
Step 5: Realization	Individual	Mental practice in competition; pre-start competition support:
	10–15 × 3–5 min	Planning competition versions
	10–15 × 5–10 min	Recovery between matches
	10–15 × 1–3 min	Concentration before matches
	10–15 × 5–10 min	Self-examination after competition with VCR analysis

*Homework for steps 1–3: mental relaxation with music; special relaxation program with portable GSR_{BFB}; 10–15 times × 10–15 min.
Daily relaxation practice with portable GSR_{BFB} and EMG_{BFB}; extended relaxation 4–5 times × 15 min; brief relaxation 7–10 times × 5 min; brief relaxation 10–12 times × 1 min.

Table 4.8 outlines the general principles of a mental training program (based on the five-step approach) developed for and applied to Israeli elite combat sport athletes (judo, wrestling, taekwondo). This is derived from extensive experience with athletes successfully participating in top-level events such as the Olympic Games and the World and European Championships. Table 4.9 presents an example of an

Table 4.9 General pre-competition weekly mental training program (combat sport)

Sunday	Monday	Tuesday	Wednesday	Thursday	Friday	Saturday
At the end of training extended relaxation with music accompanied with portable GSR_{BFB}—10–15 min	In training situation: Concentration exercises in warm-up with portable EMG_{BFB}+ IM fragments of competition matches (excitation and concentration)—$1–2 \times 2–3$ min Muscle relaxation and rest between fights—2–3 min Brief relaxation after training with portable GSR_{BFB} – 5 min	Homework with portable GSR_{BFB} and analysis of VCR films collecting with competition fights—$3–4 \times 5–10$ min	In training: Relaxation + imagery (excitation part) with concentration on concrete competition fight and next relaxation (EMG—0.8–0.9 μV): 1×5 min; 1×3 min; 1×1 min ("double feedback") Mental recovery after training (group) with portable GSR_{BFB}—5–10 min	In training: Concentration exercises $1–2 \times 1–3$ min Imagery with portable GSR_{BFB} before fights—$2–3 \times 1$ min Relaxation after training with portable GSR_{BFB}—5–10 min	In training: Brief relaxation during athlete's performance (special exercises) $2–3 \times 30$ s $2–3\times 10$ s Homework with portable GSR_{BFB}—brief relaxation: $3–4 \times 1$ min	Homework: Preview and analyzing competition and training fights (VCR collection program) Brief relaxation with GSR_{BFB}—5–10 min

approximate, general precompetition weekly mental training program applied to elite Israeli combat sport athletes based on steps 4 and 5 of the entire program.

Next, a concrete example of an individual precompetition biofeedback (BFB) training plan with a specifically prepared VCR collection of previous competitions is presented (for a wrestler participating in an event which took place in July):

30 June BFB training with GSR, relaxation: twice × 3 min.
BFB training with GSR and audiovisual stimulation (athlete listens to competition noise from last world championship): 3–5 min. Preview of his previous match (Israel–China; score 3:6) and thus relaxation with GSR_{BFB} and imagining competition fragments of this match with corrections, following analysis of this fight together with coach and sport psychologist.

2 July Relaxation with $EMG–GSR_{BFB}$ accompanied with a special music program: 15 min (EMG from baseline to 0.8–0.9 μV).
Homework with VCR collection film (special exercises).

5 July BFB training with EMG (from baseline to 0.6–0.9 μV): 2–3 × 1–3 min.
BFB training with GSR, relaxation–excitation (imagining competition fragments): twice × 5 min (last time with "double feedback").
Preview of his competition match (Israel–Poland; score 4:2) and imagery based on this match, including corrections and planning.
Relaxation with GSR_{BFB} 3–5 min: preparation for next match (Israel–USA) and imagining this match with GSR_{BFB} and competition noise from VCR program.
Analysis of this fight together with coach.
Relaxation with GSR_{BFB}: 5 min.

6 July BFB training with portable GSR, relaxation–excitation–relaxation: 3 × 3 min.
Preview of competition match (Israel–USA; score 0:1) and imagery based on this match, including corrections and planning.

7 July Relaxation exercises with portable GSR twice × 5–10 min at the end of training. Homework with VCR collection film.

One underlying principle of the five-step mental preparation program presented in this chapter is to guide the athlete through situations with a gradual increase in difficulty or complexity, both across and within steps. With accumulating success in coping with increasingly problematic situations, the athlete's self-confidence may increase based on his or her increased levels of experienced self-efficacy (Bandura, 1997). It should be noted that in the long run, the increased probability of success in competitions following a systematic application of the program is expected to produce a positive momentum for the athlete's performance, as well as a decreased crisis probability (Bar-Eli, 1997).

The five-step mental preparation program involves a substantial number of sessions intended to allow mastery of the various techniques and achieve a practical payoff. To motivate athletes to adhere to this protocol, we followed the principles suggested by the cognitive behavior modification approach (Meichenbaum, 1977). According to this approach, the key to motivation and cooperation in any training involves the presentation of a "face valid" program. Without awareness of the program's relevance and without confidence in the program, positive change cannot take place. Accordingly, this program enables the athlete to follow vividly his or her own progress and to experience success not only in the laboratory but also in the field. As a result, the athlete undergoing such a program has a greater tendency to adhere to and benefit from it.

In principle, the entire program can be tailored to a competitive season of an internationally active elite athlete such as a judoka, wrestler, fencer, swimmer, or windsurfer, who may have had little previous experience with similar mental preparation programs. In the subsequent season, following a break from competition and training, the same athlete may restart with an abridged version of steps 1 and 2 to refresh his or her knowledge and rapidly progress through steps 3–5. When the sport psychologist is not available (e.g., when the athlete participates in long training camps abroad), the athlete may use written instructions that have been prepared in advance by the sport psychologist and practice the technique under the supervision of the coach.

The number of sessions in each step of the program was derived from previous research and experience with the program (Blumenstein, Bar-Eli, & Tenenbaum, 1995), although some modifications to the length of the program may be needed to take into account particular characteristics of the sport and the athlete.

It could be argued that, on the practical level, the requirement to collect VCR data on the performer across a wide variety of competitive settings that differ in their perceived importance to the athlete may limit the viability of this type of intervention. However, the cumulative experience of the authors in applying this program with elite athletes has provided consistent positive outcomes and satisfaction in participating athletes and, thus, has further strengthened the program's effectiveness.

EFFECTIVE BIOFEEDBACK INTERVENTIONS: ENSURING CAUSATION

The five-step approach certainly offers an excellent structure for the effective application of biofeedback. However, one factor that needs careful consideration is causation: does the pattern of activity that has been measured (or, in the case of biofeedback, promoted) cause the performance effect that you see? This is an important component of the second step, Interpretation (see chapter 2), and is a particularly crucial consideration due to the individual variation that may occur. An example from our own experience illustrates this, and we are indebted to our colleagues Gavin Loze, Mark Bellamy, and Paul Holmes for their work in this area.

At step 2, interpretation plays a big part since mechanistic causation obviously underpins the extent to which signals can be interpreted clearly as representing the most effective biofeedback modality. However, both individual differences and the extent to which different electrode sites tell a consistent story must be considered. In an attempt to improve understanding of central concomitants of performance, and as a possible precursor to EEG biofeedback, we used a multi-site electrode montage to

Table 4.10 Group mean (SD) EEG alpha power (μV^2): anterior temporal sites (T3/T4) in elite air pistol athletes

	Left hemisphere (T3)		Right hemisphere (T4)	
	Good	Bad	Good	Bad
Epoch 1	44.45 (61.67)	55.05 (66.76)	6.72 (7.52)	8.32 (9.01)
Epoch 2	67.82 (108.14)	65.03 (120.71)	3.88 (2.67)	5.26 (5.10)
Epoch 3	51.85 (67.72)	31.72 (28.88)	4.76 (4.37)	3.81 (2.26)

examine activity in the moments approaching trigger pull in elite air-pistol athletes (Loze, Holmes, Collins, Shaw, & Bellamy, in review). Athletes' EEG activity was examined throughout a 60-shot simulated match, and analysis focused on three 2-s epochs immediately prior to each shot.

Group data for the six shooters involved showed similar effects to those found by different studies in a variety of sports. Examinations of archery (Salazar, Landers, Petruzzell, Crews, Kubitz, & Han, 1990), shooting (Hatfield, Landers, & Ray, 1984, 1987; Landers, Han, Salazar, Petruzzell, Kubitz, & Gannon, 1994) and golf (Crews & Landers, 1993) have consistently found greater levels of alpha power in left hemisphere than in right hemisphere sites. Our data, shown in Table 4.10, demonstrate this effect and also show an even stronger trend in good rather than bad shots. The effect is particularly marked in the final 2 s before trigger pull, an effect which has also been highlighted by the previous investigations.

Whilst this group data approach is rather traditional, it does offer a means of comparing our data with those from other investigations. Based on these and the previous data, the practitioner *may* conclude that the greater left hemisphere alpha activity was in some way "causing" the good performance and hence initiate a biofeedback intervention designed to promote this change. Such a conclusion, even though "correlation does not prove causation," would be tenable since (a) groups of better performers consistently show this effect, and (b) within-subject comparisons suggest it as a discriminant factor in performance outcome.

Consideration of some other electrode sites supports this view. A similar pattern of alpha activity was also found at the modified central sites (C3′/C4′), with significantly greater power at the left than at to the right sites, regardless of pre-shot epoch or shot quality. When combined, the results appear supportive of a general hemispheric difference. However, no such effect was apparent at other pairs of sites (F3–F4 and P3–P4) whilst at posterior temporal sites (T5–T6, see Table 4.11) the effect was reversed, with greater alpha activity at the right hemisphere site (T6).

The point is that the apparently simple causative relationship between left hemisphere alpha activity and performance is, perhaps not surprisingly, far more complex than at first sight. The essential step of interpretation (cf. Chapter 2) does offer some assistance, however. T3 and C3′ are both close to two well-established areas of the cerebral cortex known to be involved in dialogue, namely Broca's area and Wernicke's area (see Kolb & Wishaw, 1995). Thus, the interpretation of "greater self-talk

Table 4.11 Group mean (SD) EEG alpha power (μV^2): posterior temporal sites (T5/T6)

	Left hemisphere (T5)		Right hemisphere (T6)	
	Good	Bad	Good	Bad
Epoch 1	5.66 (4.82)	8.54 (5.10)	16.96 (29.92)	24.45 (47.90)
Epoch 2	6.17 (6.38)	6.09 (4.04)	22.98 (48.21)	16.28 (25.13)
Epoch 3	7.45 (6.28)	5.72 (3.61)	26.33 (54.17)	10.39 (15.62)

(and hence less alpha) = lower performance," an idea originally proposed by Hatfield et al. in 1984 (but challenged by Lawton, Hung, Saarela, & Hatfield, 1998), may well be the causative interpretation which offers the way forwards. So, once again, biofeedback to increase left hemisphere alpha activity would seem to be the correct course of action.

Two factors merit consideration however; one individual and one interpretative. Examination of individual athlete profiles (an important concern which is discussed later in this section) show that the self-talk approach does not apply to all. Consider the profile for subject three from our study, presented in Figure 4.3.

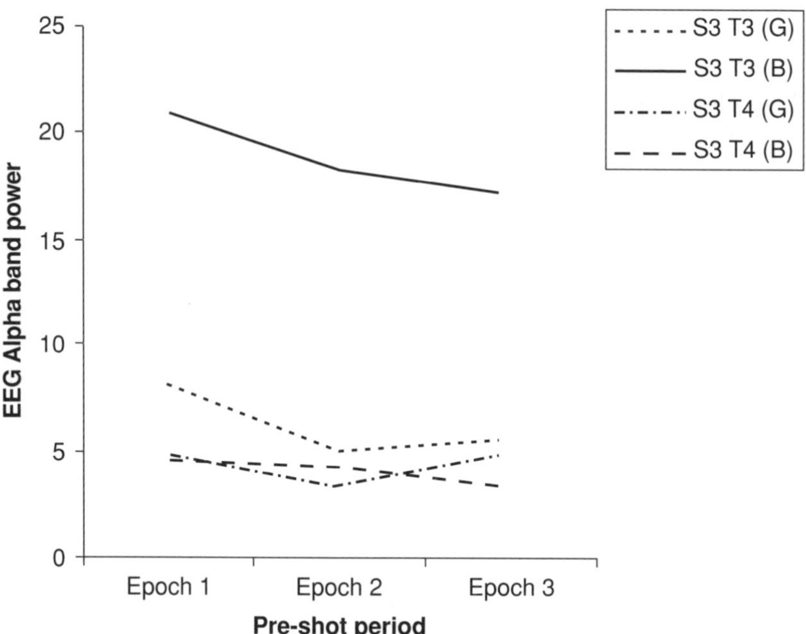

Figure 4.3 Profile of mean EEG alpha band power at T_3 and T_4 for subject 3 (S3) during good (G) and bad (B) performance

In stimulated recall interviews (an important feature in planning effective biofeedback interventions), this athlete reported that he liked to use self-talk as a part of his competition strategy. *His* perception was that less self-talk was associated with worse performance. Examination of his EEG profile against performance showed this to be so. Higher left hemisphere alpha activity was associated with poor performance—the opposite effect to that suggested by the group data. Subsequent checks showed that this athlete had the same regional specialization as the other athletes (a left hemisphere speech area), so the effect observed was genuine rather than due to some brain-related structural difference. Pursuit of the biofeedback strategy indicated by group data might well have caused a performance drop for this individual.

The second factor relates to the veracity, or at least the explanative power, of the self-talk hypothesis. Consider the posterior temporal data (T5–T6). The posterior temporal areas of the cortex are implicated in the secondary processing of "form-based" spatial information transmitted along the ventral stream from the occipital cortex (Goodale & Milner, 1992). Thus, the data are supportive of greater secondary visual processing in the left hemisphere—all these athletes were right-eyed and, as is fairly standard in this sport, actually wore a patch over their left eye. The significantly higher right hemisphere alpha power in good shots suggests that an explicit de-emphasis on left eye activity is advisable. Once again, it would appear that a biofeedback intervention targeted at a simple increase in left hemisphere alpha would not automatically cause an improvement in performance. The message is clear: take a lot of trouble to check that what you are trying to change will actually cause the effect you require.

Of course, without painstaking longitudinal study, no one can tell whether an intervention aimed at modifying EEG style to fit an "established norm" would improve all these athletes' performance. In the short term, however, blanket application of the accepted position might well have disrupted the performance of those who displayed the greatest differences from this state. The message is clear. Careful checks should play their part in all biofeedback interventions if you are to avoid the potential for damage which results from individual variation from the norm, or from errors made in deciding what the norm is!

These data have, hopefully, stressed the importance of checking the nature of psychophysiological concomitants for each individual before attempting to apply them. It is important to recognize that this process can benefit substantially from the consideration of several factors in tandem, focusing on the ways in which these factors offer a more elaborate consistent picture or a contrasting story. This is known as a "triangulation of measures approach." Thus, in the pistol study presented earlier, EEG, HR, respiration, and performance data were collected in addition to ongoing mental task load and qualitative data throughout a simulated match (cf. step 3 of the five-step approach). Additionally, however, video recordings of the athlete's face during performance, in conjunction with performance data, were used to generate stimulated recall data which, together with other self-reported information, was then fitted to the full picture. Integration of these different data sources offers a much richer picture and enables the accurate focusing of biofeedback techniques to each individual.

A lack of awareness strategy is recognized by most athletes involved, and the development of this "in the zone" state is the focus of many biofeedback-based interventions. However, consider data from another study (Bellamy, Collins, Holmes, Loze, & Hooper, in review), which examined archers' pre-shot psychophysiological state. Several of the participants in this study seemed unable to implement this state. In fact, further discussion revealed subtle but significant differences in their self-reported focus. Consider this archer whose EEG results demonstrated a consistently high T3 power throughout the pre-shot cycle.

Good shooting
Usually there are some times I'm not aware. Erm, the first time I experienced this was way back in 1975 and I shot 1170, which was about 90 points higher than I've ever shot before. I know what happens when I do get the feeling. I know it's a subconscious, it's total subconscious that takes over.

Bad shooting
As soon as it gets to a certain stage, the timing's not good, then the brain switches on; you know, the conscious mind will come on and say "cut!" you know – "abort! stop!"

In contrast, consider the positive focus strategy for two other archers, both of whom did poorly, were of a lower level, and displayed very haphazard occipital EEG with low T3 power.

Positive focus
Well you know we had clicks on bows, yeah? And it's a, you know ... an automatic reaction—that goes and we shoot. And it's just a condition reflex really. Erm, unless you absolutely concentrate 100%; if you're not quite with it, then, you know, sometimes you can shoot on another person's clicker. Or, if there's people clicking cameras and that, it can just give you a bit of a jump.

Positive focus
When there's a day where things are happening, whether you're getting anxious; you're thinking of some big shot—whatever—then I start using: relax the hands ... relax the hands.

Now consider the two best athletes in the entire sample, who both displayed very small shot-related EEG changes, limited to the final 2 s before arrow release. These athletes report a strategy which keeps them in the right condition for as long as possible. No cycle exists around the shot per se; rather each shot is a part of a larger 'macro' cycle.

Shooter F
You are very focused on what you are doing—you are not conscious of anything else.

Shooter E
Once you are in the groove you shoot . . . again and again. No change, no thought, just shoot.

These last two subjects exhibit patterns which fit well with the attention–intention switch highlighted in Chapter 2 and the self-report data support the nature of this change. The bottom line of all these data is that the correct mental set *can* be identified with increasing accuracy by the psychophysiological concomitants of self-reported mental set. Consequently, biofeedback interventions can be implemented, on an individual basis, with faith in the veracity of the changes that the interventions are attempting to generate.

SUMMARY

Chapter 4 focuses on the major area of performance enhancement, and particularly on mental preparation with biofeedback training programs. The goals of the two biofeedback training programs presented in this chapter are to improve the athletic self-regulation training level, optimize competitive behavior, and enhance athletic performance. These programs are based on research findings and have revealed many potential options for practical work in various sports. Two biofeedback approaches attempted to come out of the laboratory framework into the field. However, it is clear that both training programs demand special biofeedback devices and knowledge in the area of sport psychology, psychophysiology, and sport training. Finally, the chapter points out some of the limitations of the biofeedback approach.

Biofeedback can provide rapid and immediately available information about the athlete's physiology and psychological states, which will maximize athletic skills and subsequently competition results. However, for various reasons (e.g., the expense of the devices, lack of knowledge about psychophysiology among coaches, orientation of biofeedback training in the laboratory setting which is far from "real life" and therefore difficult for athletes and coaches to accept), biofeedback applications to modern sport are still in their infancy and are not yet a regular part of the training process. Therefore, we believe that biofeedback applications have great potential in the field of sport, and we hope that our chapter has contributed in this direction.

REFERENCES

Bandura, A. (1997). *Self-efficacy: The exercise of control.* New York: Freeman.

Bar-Eli, M. (1985). Arousal-performance relationship: A transactional view on performance jags. *International Journal of Sport Psychology*, **16**, 193–209.

Bar-Eli, M. (1997). Psychological performance crisis in competition, 1984–1996: A review. *European Yearbook of Sport Psychology*, **1**, 1, 73–112.

Bar-Eli, M., & Tenenbaum, G. (1989). Coach–psychologist relations in competitive sport. *The Journal of Applied Research in Coaching and Athletics*, **4**, 150–156.

Bar-Eli, M., Tenenbaum, G., & Elbaz, G. (1989). Prestart susceptibility to psychological crisis in competitive sport: Theory and research. *International Journal of Sport Psychology*, **20**, 13–30.

Bellamy, M. B., Collins, D., Holmes, P., Loze, G., & Hooper, H. (2001). Shot timing within the cardiac cycle of UIT air-pistol shooters and archers. *The Sport Psychologist* (in review).

Blumenstein, B. (1999). Mental training with biofeedback in combat sport. In V. Hosek, P. Tilinger, & L. Bilek (eds.), *Proceedings of the Xth European Congress of Sport Psychology, Part 1* (pp. 119–121). Prague, Czech Republic: Charles University.

Blumenstein, B., & Bar-Eli, M. (1998). Self-regulation training with biofeedback in elite canoers and kayakers. In V. Issurin (ed.), *Science and practice of canoe/kayak high performance training* (pp. 124–132). Netanya, Israel: Wingate Institute.

Blumenstein, B., & Bar-Eli, M. (2001). A five-step approach for biofeedback training in sport. *Sportwissenschaft*, 31(4), 412–424.

Blumenstein, B., Bar-Eli, M., & Tenenbaum, G. (1995). The augmenting role of biofeedback: Effects of autogenic, imagery, and music training on physiological indices and athletic performance. *Journal of Sports Sciences*, **13**, 343–354.

Blumenstein, B., Bar-Eli, M., & Tenenbaum, G. (1997). A five-step approach to mental training incorporating biofeedback. *The Sport Psychologist*, **11**, 440–453.

Blumenstein, B., Tenenbaum, G., Bar-Eli, M., & Pie, J. (1995). Mental preparation techniques with elite athletes using computerized biofeedback and VCR. In W. K. Simpson, A. D. Le Unes, & J. S. Picou (eds.), *Applied research in coaching and athletics annual* (pp. 1–15). Boston, MA: American Press.

Bompa, T. (1994). *Theory and methodology of training: The key to athletic performance* (3rd ed.). Dubuque, IA: Kendall/Hunt.

Crews, D. J., & Landers, D.M. (1993). Electroencephalographic measures of attentional patterns prior to the golf putt.*Medicine and Science in Sports and Exercise*, **25**, 116–126.

Eklund, R. C., Gould, D., & Jackson, S. A. (1993). Psychological foundations of Olympic wrestling excellence: Reconciling individual differences and nonathletic characterization. *Journal of Applied Sport Psychology*, **5**, 35–47.

Goodale, M. A. & Milner, A. D. (1992). Separate pathways for perception and action. *Trends in Neuroscience*, **15**, 20–25.

Hatfield, B. D., Landers, D. M., & Ray, W. J. (1984). Cognitive processes during self-paced motor performance: an electroencephalographic profile of skilled marksmen. *Journal of Sport Psychology*, **6**, 42–59.

Hatfield, B. D., Landers, D. M., & Ray, W. J. (1987). Cardiovascular–CNS interactions during a self-paced, intentional attentive state: Elite marksmanship performance. *Psychophysiology*, **24**, 542–549.

Highlen, P., Bennett, B. (1979). Psychological characteristics of successful and nonsuccessful elite wrestlers: An exploratory study. *Journal of Sport Psychology*, **1**, 123–137.

Kolb, B., & Wishaw, I. Q. (1995). *Fundamentals of human neuropsychology*. New York: W. H. Freeman & Co.

Kondo, C., Canter, J., & Bean, J. (1977). Intersession interval and reductions in frontalis EMG during biofeedback training. *Psychophysiology*, **1**, 15–17.

Landers, D., Petruzzello, S., Slazar, W., Crews, D., Kubitz, K., Gannon, T., & Han, M. (1991). The influence of electrocortical biofeedback on performance in pre-elite archers. *Medicine and Science in sport and exercise*, **23**, 123–129.

Landers, D. M., & Hunt, K. J., (1988). *Shooting sports research.* The Education and Training Division. National Rifle Association of America. Washington, D.C.

Landers, D. M., Han, M., Salazar, W., Petruzzello, S. J., Kubitz, K. A., & Gannon, T. L. (1994). Effects of learning on electroencephalographic and electrocardiographic patterns in novice archers. *International Journal of Sport Psychology*, **25**, 313–330.

Lawton, G. W., Hung, T. M., Saarela, P., & Hatfield, B. D. (1998). Electroencephalography and mental states associated with elite performance. *Journal of Sport & Exercise Psychology*, **20**, 35–53.

Loze, G. M., Holmes, P., Collins, D., Shaw, J. C., & Bellamy, M. J. B. (2001). Examining the neuropsychological mechanisms underlying UIT air-pistol shooting performance. *International Journal of Sport Psychology*. (in review)

Meichenbaum, D. (1977). *Cognitive behavior modification.* New York: Plenum.

Nowicki, D. (1989). Mental preparation for competition: A study based upon Asian combat sports. In J. Kremer & W. Crawford (eds.), *The psychology of sport: Theory and practice* (pp. 26–31). Belfast: Queen's University of Belfast.

Salazar, W., Landers, D. M., Petruzzello, S. J., Crews, D. J., Kubitz, K. A., & Han, M. (1990). Hemispheric asymmetry, cardiac response, and performance in elite archers. *Research Quarterly for Exercise and Sport*, **61**, 351–359.

Schultz, I. H. (1970). Das autogene training (Autogenic training). Stuttgart, Germany: Thieme.

Vanek, M., & Cratty, B. J. (1970). *Psychology and the superior athlete.* New York: Macmillan.

Zaichkowsky, L., & Takenaka, K. (1993). Optimizing arousal level. In R. N. Singer, M. Murphey, & L. K. Tennant (eds.), *Handbook of research on sport psychology* (pp. 511–527). New York: Macmillan.

CHAPTER 5

Biofeedback in Exercise Psychology

Panteleimon Ekkekakis and Steven J. Petruzzello

INTRODUCTION

Exercise psychology is concerned primarily with the psychological changes that accompany acute and chronic exercise and the psychological processes that underlie the participation in and adherence to exercise programs. Unlike sport psychology, the populations typically involved in exercise psychology research are nonathletic and the objective is not the enhancement of athletic performance, but rather the promotion of health and well-being.

Most of the studies on the use of biofeedback techniques in the context of exercise were conducted in the late 1970s and early 1980s (see earlier reviews by Petruzzello, Landers, & Salazar, 1991; Zaichkowsky & Fuchs, 1988). For reasons that we will examine shortly, the interest in biofeedback within exercise psychology has since been on the decline. This is unfortunate, however, because, as we will attempt to demonstrate, biofeedback techniques may provide effective solutions to some important problems encountered in health- and well-being-oriented exercise programs. In this chapter, we will (a) examine the reasons for the reduced interest in biofeedback within exercise psychology in recent years, (b) establish a rationale for the use of biofeedback in exercise settings, (c) review the research literature on the effectiveness of biofeedback for regulating exercise intensity, and (d) propose some future directions.

From a practical standpoint, the greatest challenge facing researchers in exercise psychology today is increasing the rates of public participation in and adherence to exercise programs. Evidence from a growing number of epidemiological and experimental studies shows that regular exercise is associated with a host of important health benefits [United States Department of Health and Human Services (USDHHS), 1996]. Yet the rates of public participation in exercise programs remain low and the rates of dropout remain high. Specifically, in the United States, the 1998–1999 progress review of the Healthy People 2000 program showed that only 23% of adults engage in

Brain and Body in Sport and Exercise: Biofeedback Applications in Performance Enhancement.
Edited by Boris Blumenstein, Michael Bar-Eli, and Gershon Tenenbaum.

light-to-moderate physical activity five times per week and only 16% engage in light-to-moderate physical activity seven times per week (United States National Center for Health Statistics, 1999). Both figures have remained virtually unchanged since 1985 (22% and 16%, respectively) and both fall short of the targets for the year 2000 (30% for both categories). Furthermore, about half of the people who initiate an exercise program are likely to drop out within the first six months, while cognitive and behavioral interventions designed to increase the rates of participation and adherence typically meet with limited success (Dishman & Buckworth, 1996).

Traditionally, the problem of exercise involvement and adherence has been approached from a social-cognitive perspective (USDHHS, 1996). From this perspective, exercise participation is explained through such variables as attitudes, subjective norms, or self-perceptions. However, other perspectives may also help shed some light on this issue. As a case in point, research in general psychology has shown that the affect experienced in a situation is a good predictor of the amount of time people subsequently choose to spend in that situation (Emmons & Diener, 1986). In simple terms, in exercise, as in other domains, people are likely to do what makes them feel good and avoid what makes them feel bad. Why is this observation relevant to the issue of biofeedback? There is growing evidence that the intensity of exercise is closely associated with people's affective responses to the exercise. Specifically, it has been shown that increases in exercise intensity are linked to declines in affective valence (Acevedo, Rinehardt, & Kraemer, 1994; Hardy & Rejeski, 1989; Parfitt & Eston, 1995; Parfitt, Eston, & Connolly, 1996; Parfitt, Markland, & Holmes, 1994; see Ekkekakis & Petruzzello, 1999, for a review). Although a clear relationship between affective responses and exercise adherence remains to be established, it is noteworthy that studies have also shown an inverse relationship between exercise intensity and adherence (Epstein, Koeske, & Wing, 1984; Lee, Jensen, Oberman, Fletcher, Fletcher, & Raczynski, 1996; Sallis, Haskell, Fortmann, Vranizan, Taylor, & Solomon, 1986).

Consistent with these findings, recent physical activity recommendations have called for moderate-intensity activities. According to the National Institutes of Health Development Panel on Physical Activity and Cardiovascular Health (National Institutes of Health, 1996), such activities are recommended because they are "more likely to be continued than are high-intensity activities" (p. 243). Similarly, according to the newly issued Healthy People 2010 program, "each person should recognize that starting out slowly with an activity that is enjoyable and gradually increasing the frequency and duration of the activity is central to the adoption and maintenance of physical activity behavior" (USDHHS, 2000, p. 22–4). At the same time, however, as several authors have pointed out, starting out "too slow" may entail a substantial time commitment with negligible fitness or health benefits (Lee, Hsieh, & Paffenbarger, 1995; Morris, 1996; Winett, 1998). Individuals who begin an exercise program typically have high expectations of fitness and health benefits, which, if not met, may lead to disappointment (Desharnais, Bouillon, & Godin, 1986) and, eventually, to disengagement from exercise.

The problem is that individuals beginning an exercise program for the first time cannot be expected to know what constitutes a "slow" start or an appropriate progression.

Research has shown that most people are not intuitively (i.e., without training) capable of accurate self-monitoring and self-regulation of exercise intensity (Kollenbaum, 1994; Kollenbaum, Dahme, & Kirchner, 1996; Kosiek, Szymanski, Lox, Kelley, & MacFarlane, 1999). For example, Kollenbaum (1994) found that approximately 40% of cardiac patients undergoing exercise rehabilitation underestimated their heart rate, while about 10% overestimated it. Kosiek et al. (1999) found that, despite reporting similar levels of perceived exertion, 16% of cardiac rehabilitation patients exceeded their target heart rates, 67% fell short, and only 20% were within the target range. An underestimation of the appropriate range of exercise training intensity may result in overexertion, risk of injury or cardiovascular complications (Dishman, 1994), increases in the perceived aversiveness of exercise (Brewer, Manos, McDevitt, Cornelius, & Van Raalte, 2000), and, eventually, the discontinuation of the exercise program. On the other hand, an overestimation may deprive the exerciser of many of the potential benefits of the exercise program, thus possibly leading to frustration and drop-out.

For these reasons, it is critical that exercise be performed within a range of intensity that maximizes the health and fitness benefits (through the proper application of the training principles of overload and progression) without being experienced as aversive and without creating a risk for injury or cardiovascular problems. Biofeedback can be of great value in achieving these objectives. According to our conceptual model, in healthy populations (Figure 5.1), the role of biofeedback is to help exercisers improve their ability to self-monitor and self-regulate the intensity of their effort. By doing so, it is assumed that they will be able to regulate the level of perceived exertion and thus the valence of the affective responses that they experience. In turn, this is expected to contribute to an enhancement of the sense of enjoyment and satisfaction that the participants derive from the exercise experience. Ultimately, this should lead to improved adherence rates. In clinical populations (Figure 5.2) suffering from exercise-limiting conditions (e.g., exertion-induced angina, exertion-induced asthma, dyspnea due to

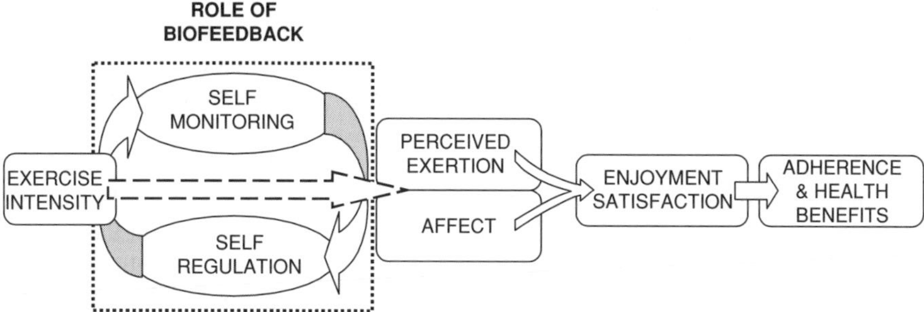

Figure 5.1 Conceptual model for the role of biofeedback in exercise for healthy populations. By improving the self-monitoring and self-regulation of exercise intensity, biofeedback should allow exercisers to control the level of perceived exertion and affective valence that they experience. In turn, this should lead to more enjoyment and satisfaction and, ultimately, to improved exercise adherence rates.

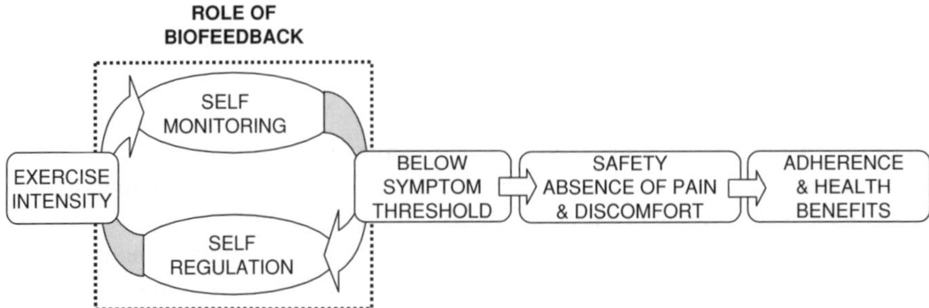

Figure 5.2 Conceptual model for the role of biofeedback in exercise for clinical populations with exercise-limiting conditions (e.g., exertion-induced angina, exertion-induced asthma, dyspnea due to chronic obstructive pulmonary disease, pain due to arterial claudication, etc.). By improving the self-monitoring and self-regulation of exercise intensity, biofeedback should allow patients to maintain a level of exercise intensity that is below the threshold that elicits unpleasant or dangerous symptoms. This should improve the safety and reduce the aversiveness of exercise, thus encouraging patients to remain physically active.

chronic obstructive pulmonary disease, pain due to arterial claudication, etc.), biofeedback may be an effective method of teaching patients to recognize some early warning signs or symptoms. By doing so, the patients may be able to maintain the level of exercise intensity below the threshold that elicits unpleasant or dangerous symptoms.

WHY THE INATTENTION TO BIOFEEDBACK WITHIN EXERCISE PSYCHOLOGY?

The inattention toward biofeedback in exercise psychology is a reflection of the theoretical perspectives that have prevailed in this scientific field during the 30 or so years of its evolution. The perceptions of exertion and the affective responses that accompany exercise participation have been mainly examined from the perspective of cognitive and social-cognitive theories. The common theme that characterizes these approaches is that human experiences are formed in and, therefore, depend on the mind. The body is believed to provide the mind with raw sensory data but these data do not influence human experience directly. It is only when this information is evaluated through a cognitive filter (for example, a cognitive appraisal of threat, self-presentation, self-efficacy, etc.) that it acquires some significance for the person. Importantly, these filters are considered so powerful that they are believed to be capable of transforming sensory data into very diverse experiences. Consequently, according to these theories, since the mind is what determines the experience, the most effective way of changing the experience is through changing the cognitive processes that occur in the mind. Therefore, biofeedback, a process intended to improve the self-monitoring and self-regulation of bodily functions, is regarded as being of relatively little consequence.

For example, according to Averill (1980), "it is . . . worth emphasizing that [bodily] feedback is subject to second-order monitoring . . . and it is the monitoring that determines the quality of experience, not the feedback per se" (p. 317). Similarly, Bandura (1982) asserted that physiological input "is not inherently enlightening" and can acquire meaning "only through cognitive appraisal" (p. 127). Lazarus has expressed similar ideas. In his view, the physiological input is similar to malleable raw material. Depending on the cognitive interpretation, it can be transformed into diametrically opposite experiences. Using running as an example to illustrate his point, Lazarus (1991) stated that the physiological cues associated with running-induced fatigue can be experienced as distress in a close race because they are interpreted as signs of exhaustion, thus raising the possibility that the race may be lost. However, the same physiological cues may lead to a sense of satisfaction during training because they signify that the body is being strengthened without much being at stake. Thus, it is not surprising that, commenting on the use of biofeedback for emotional regulation, Lazarus (1975, 1977) contended that biofeedback is merely "dealing with the somatic reaction rather than its cause" (Lazarus, 1975, p. 559), whereas the use of cognitive coping strategies constitutes "direct action" that can regulate emotional arousal by actively coping with the appraisals that generated the arousal "in the first place" (p. 559).

These views have been widely echoed within exercise psychology. Authors have commonly suggested that, in order to cope with the intense and unpleasant physiological symptoms associated with strenuous exercise, individuals should try to cognitively "reinterpret" (e.g., McAuley, 1994) or "reframe" (e.g., Hardy & Rejeski, 1989) these symptoms in their minds.

These ideas seem to promote the separation of the mind from the body and, as a result, they have been criticized as dualistic. For example, according to Lee (1995), Bandura's position that physiological activity only acquires meaning after it is cognitively analyzed and interpreted, effectively reduces the individual to "a collection of subjective experiences, with a body more or less tacked on as a way of getting around" (pp. 261–262). Similarly, within exercise psychology, Morgan (1989) has contended that many authors, "especially those who rely exclusively on cognitive psychology, seem to believe that the head does not have a body" (p. 100).

TIME FOR INTEGRATION?

On the one hand, the studies that have been based on cognitive and social-cognitive theories have offered strong evidence that attention and cognition are important determinants of perceptions of exertion and affective responses to exercise. On the other hand, it would be groundless to refute the importance of physiological input in shaping subjective responses to a *physical* activity, such as exercise. As Brownell (1991) put it, "control over our bodies must be considered within the context of biological realities" (p. 308). Therefore, the challenge lies in developing a conceptual framework that reflects the importance of both cognitive and interoceptive factors and outlines the conditions for their interaction.

A model of perceived exertion proposed by Rejeski (1981) was the first attempt at such an integration. According to this model, the relative influence of cognitive factors and physiological input in shaping perceptions of exertion varies systematically across increasing "doses" of exercise. Specifically, "cognitive variables should be expected to influence [perceived exertion] most when the sport/physical task in question is performed at, or has physiological demands of, a submaximal nature" (p. 314). Beyond this submaximal level, "there is a point in the physical stress of exercise at which sensory cues, due to their strength, dominate perception. Under such conditions, it is unreasonable to expect mediation by psychological factors" (Rejeski, 1985, p. 372). It is unreasonable because "powerful metabolic changes may preclude cognitive manipulations from enabling someone to continue an activity" (Rejeski & Thompson, 1993, p. 18). Considerable empirical evidence has accumulated over the years in support of this idea. For instance, the expectation of a longer versus a shorter exercise duration was shown to lead to significantly lower perceptions of exertion up to the 15th minute, but not during the final 5 min of a demanding 20-min run at 85% of maximal aerobic capacity (Rejeski & Ribisl, 1980). Also, contrary to what was seen with exercise at 60% and 75% of maximal heart rate, attentional manipulations by means of music and sensory deprivation had no effects on perceptions of exertion at 85% of maximal heart rate (Boutcher & Trenske, 1990). Similarly, the presence of a coactor appeared to be associated with suppressed perceptions of exertion at 25% and 50%, but not at 75% of maximal aerobic capacity (Hardy, Hall, and Prestholdt, 1986).

The conceptual approach taken in the present review is generally consistent with the postulates of Rejeski's (1981) model. Specifically, we believe that exertional and affective experiences during exercise are a function of both cognition and direct interoception (i.e., the cognitively unmediated perception of physiological functions by the brain). Although both of these ingredients are necessary, we also believe that the relative importance of these two factors changes as a function of exercise intensity. Specifically, we speculate that cognition plays the primary role in low and moderate exercise intensities and direct interoception becomes the dominant influence at high and near-maximal intensities.

As noted earlier, research on exercise-induced affect has shown that, as exercise intensity increases, there are systematic declines in affective valence. Furthermore, it is noteworthy that, although interindividual variability in ratings of affective valence tends to be large at moderate and moderately high exercise intensities, it is suppressed considerably when the intensity approaches the individuals' functional limits (Hall, Ekkekakis, & Petruzzello, 2002). In these situations, there is a universally negative affective response.

From a practical standpoint, the challenge, as we see it, is to educate exercisers, particularly those who are just beginning an exercise program and are "interoceptively naive," to recognize the early signs of physiological strain and to self-regulate the intensity of their efforts accordingly. This is necessary given the fact that, beyond this level of intensity, the capacity to alter the nature of subjective experiences through cognitive coping methods is progressively reduced. In our view, biofeedback can play a significant role in this regard by sharpening the individuals' sense of interoceptive acuity.

SEEKING THE OPTIMAL EXERCISE INTENSITY FOR FITNESS, ENJOYMENT, AND ADHERENCE

Before deciding to use biofeedback to train exercisers to self-monitor and self-regulate the intensity of their efforts, one is faced with a key question: what is the optimal level of exercise intensity? In other words, what are the elusive signs of physiological strain that novice exercisers should be taught to recognize? In selecting the "optimal" level of exercise intensity for healthy populations, two factors must be considered and balanced: the need for effective training and the need to avoid aversive experiences (i.e., excessive levels of perceived exertion and negative affective responses). There is converging evidence from the physiological and the psychological literatures that the point of balance may be near the level of intensity associated with the transition from aerobic to anaerobic metabolism (referred to as the "anaerobic threshold").

First, from a *physiological* standpoint, exercising at an intensity that exceeds the anaerobic threshold has not been shown to confer any additional fitness benefits compared to exercise performed at or slightly below this threshold among previously untrained individuals (Belman & Gaesser, 1991; Weltman, Seip, Snead, Weltman, Haskvitz, Evans, Veldhuis, & Rogol, 1992). Second, from a *psychological* standpoint, preliminary studies from young and physically active participants have shown that exercising above the individually determined anaerobic threshold (defined as the ventilatory or gas exchange threshold) is associated with significant declines in the valence of affective responses (Hall et al., 2002). Studies on perceived exertion have also shown that the intensity of exercise that corresponds to the anaerobic threshold is typically rated as "somewhat hard" or "hard", whereas exercise performed at intensities below the anaerobic threshold is rated as "light" (DeMello, Cureton, Boineau, & Singh, 1987; Hetzler, Seip, Boutcher, Pierce, Snead, & Weltman, 1991; Hill, Cureton, Grisham, & Collins, 1987; Purvis & Cureton, 1981). According to Robertson (1982), on the basis of the differences in the nature and the substrates of perceived exertion, three levels of exercise intensity can be distinguished. In level I, where the metabolic rate is less than 50% $VO_{2_{max}}$, perceived exertion reflects mainly proprioception and movement awareness. Level II, where the metabolic rate is near the anaerobic threshold (i.e., 50–70% $VO_{2_{max}}$) and the ventilatory drive begins to contribute substantially to perceptions of exertion, is characterized as "uncomfortable, but tolerable." Finally, level III, where the metabolic rate exceeds the anaerobic threshold and the ventilatory drive is a very significant contributor to perceptions of exertion, is characterized as "painful or unpleasant" (Noble & Robertson, 1996, p. 395).

These observations point to some important conclusions. First, the level of exercise intensity that corresponds to the transition from aerobic to anaerobic metabolism appears to be a good candidate for a target exercise intensity, since it seems to maximize the physical training benefit without compromising affective responses, at least among

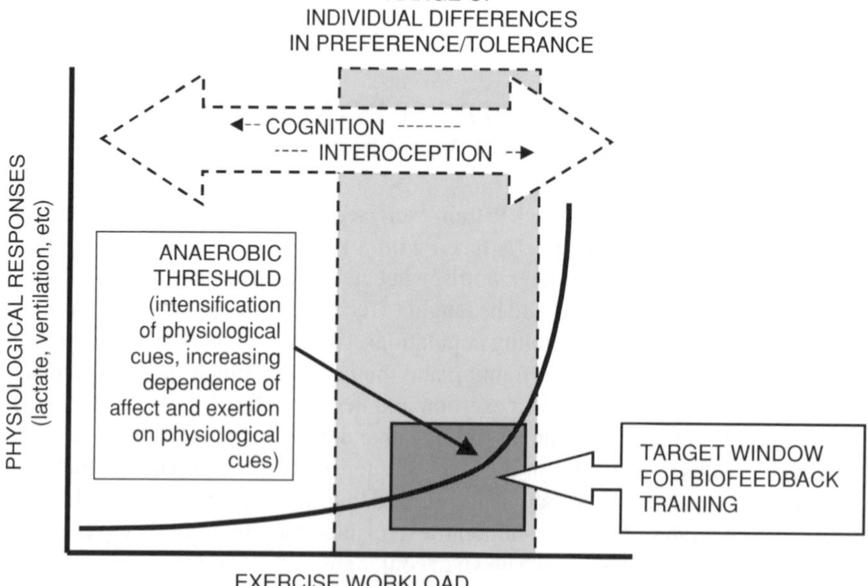

Figure 5.3 Proposed target of biofeedback training for healthy populations. Biofeedback training should be primarily aimed at teaching exercisers to recognize the transition from aerobic to anaerobic metabolism and to maintain an exercise intensity that approximates this level (within a range of individual preferences and tolerance). Beyond this level, perceived exertion and negative affective responses become progressively more dependent on physiological cues and, thus, not easily manageable through cognitive techniques.

individuals with a positive or nonnegative attitude or predisposition toward exercise. Second, the physiological, primarily ventilatory, markers of the aerobic–anaerobic transition, which become increasing salient following the transition, appear to be the most relevant candidates for biofeedback training (Figure 5.3).

PROBLEMS WITH CURRENTLY USED METHODS FOR SELF-REGULATING EXERCISE INTENSITY

When exercise is performed under expert supervision in a clinical setting, devices such as heart rate monitors (Gilman & Wells, 1993) and portable lactate analyzers (Fell, Rayfield, Gulbin, & Gaffney, 1998; Pyne, Boston, Martin, & Logan, 2000) can be used to monitor physiologic responses and guide the selection of intensity. Similarly, the development of commercial heart-rate-based servo-controlled exercise equipment (Jacobsen & Johansen, 1974; Kawada, Sunagawa, Takaki, Shishido, Miyano, Miyashita, Sato, Sugimachi, & Sunagawa, 1999; Laperriere, VanDercar, Shyu, Ward, Mc Cabe, Perry, Mosher, & Schneiderman, 1989; Pratt, Siconolfi, Webster, Hayes,

Mazzocca, & Harris, 1991) creates the possibility of automated regulation of intensity in fitness and rehabilitation centers. However, these solutions are not cost-effective and cannot be applied on a large scale. When exercise is performed in unsupervised settings, as is usually the case with healthy adults, there is a need for self-regulatory methods that are inexpensive, easy to understand and implement, and can be applied without the benefit of continuous physiological monitoring.

At present, the most frequently used methods for self-monitoring and self-regulating the intensity of physical activity are the palpation of heart beat and the use of rating scales of perceived exertion (American College of Sports Medicine, 2000). Both methods are simple and can be relatively effective, but both also have some recognized limitations.

Methods based on heart rate can be problematic due to the large inter- and intraindividual variability of submaximal heart rates (Chow & Wilmore, 1984). In addition, heart rate is a poor index of the metabolic characteristics of physical effort (i.e., whether primarily aerobic or anaerobic mechanisms are involved). For example, in a study of 20 untrained college women, Dwyer and Bybee (1983) reported that, when cycling at 75%, 80%, and 85% of heart rate reserve, 9, 13, and 15 participants, respectively, were using anaerobic metabolism, whereas the rest were using aerobic metabolism. Likewise, Katch, Weltman, Sady, and Freedson (1978) reported that, in a sample of 31 participants, when exercise was performed at 80% of maximal heart rate, 17 participants were using primarily anaerobic metabolism, whereas 14 were using primarily aerobic metabolism.

By using heart rate as a method of monitoring exercise intensity and, thus, having no information on aerobic–anaerobic balance, exercisers may inadvertently drift into anaerobic metabolism, experiencing an affectively aversive and cognitively unmanageable surge of salient interoceptive cues. Almost 20 years ago, Dwyer and Bybee (1983) recognized that this may have important implications for exercise adherence: "... compliance to a voluntary training program may be influenced by indiscriminately prescribed exercise that requires an individual to exercise considerably above his [sic] anaerobic threshold and to experience the subjective discomforts associated with exercise at that level" (p. 75).

The effectiveness of methods based on perceived exertion can also be questioned. Correlations between ratings of perceived exertion and physiological indices like oxygen uptake, heart rate, or blood lactate are often low (Potteiger & Evans, 1995; Thompson & West, 1998; Whaley & Forsyth, 1990), particularly at low and moderate levels of intensity (Borg, Ljunggren, & Ceci, 1985; Eston, Davies, & Williams, 1987; Eston & Williams, 1988; Green, Michael, & Solomon, 1999; Smutok, Skrinar, & Pandolf, 1980). This is important, given that this is the range of intensity typically prescribed to beginner exercisers. Studies have also shown that the accuracy of perceptions of exertion may change across different situations; for example, between exercise testing in a clinical setting and rehabilitation training in the field (Bayles, Metz, Robertson, Goss, Cosgrove, & McBurney, 1990; Brubaker, Rejeski, Law, Pollock, Wurst, & Miller, 1994; Gutmann, Squires, Pollock, Foster, & Anholm, 1981) or between different exercise protocols (Whaley, Woodall, Kaminsky, & Emmett, 1997).

Recognizing that, under certain conditions, ratings of exertion are not accurate indices of actual physiological effort, Dishman (1994) warned that reliance on this method may have a negative impact on exercise adherence. He asked, "How can we teach [people] to more accurately estimate and produce a prescribed exercise intensity? What is the impact of RPE errors on inactivity or on risk of injury?" (p. 1092). However, these questions remain unanswered.

BIOFEEDBACK RESEARCH IN THE CONTEXT OF EXERCISE

As noted previously, the number of studies that have examined the effectiveness of biofeedback for regulating exercise intensity is relatively small. Most of these studies have used heart rate as a biofeedback channel. This is in spite of the fact that cardiac activity is not directly accessible to conscious awareness. As several studies have shown, when asked to detect or discriminate their cardiac activity without previous training, most people perform poorly, at levels not much better than those attained by chance (see Jones, 1994, for a review).

According to Hollandsworth (1979), exercise is essentially a natural analogue to instrument-based biofeedback, as it performs the same function, namely the amplification of physiological signals, in a natural way. In fact, it has been shown that, following vigorous exercise, participants report increased awareness of their physiological state (Hollandsworth & Jones, 1979). Moreover, Jones and Hollandsworth (1981) found that the ability of physically inactive and moderately active (tennis players) participants to discriminate their cardiac activity improved (to above-chance levels) following exercise that raised their heart rates by 75% over baseline. On the other hand, highly trained male distance runners (running over 25 miles per week) did not improve their discrimination accuracy after exercise, but still faired consistently better than their inactive and moderately active counterparts both at baseline and after exercise. This finding was consistent with Hollandsworth's (1979) prediction that, by using running as a natural biofeedback, experienced runners would also be able to monitor and possibly control their physiological responses at resting conditions. However, this finding was not replicated. Montgomery, Jones, and Hollandsworth (1984) found that average-fitness participants achieved above-chance discrimination accuracy both during and after exercise (120–130 beats/min or approximately 65% of age-predicted maximal heart rate), whereas high-fitness participants achieved above-chance accuracy only after exercise. Contrary to the findings of Hollandsworth and Jones (1979), the groups did not differ at baseline. Furthermore, Montgomery et al. (1984) noted that the lower accuracy of the high-fitness group during exercise appeared to be due to inaccurate expectancies. Specifically, the high-fitness participants accepted heart rate feedback that was 30% lower than their actual heart rate as accurate on 79% of the presentations, whereas the corresponding figure for the average-fitness group was only 58%. In another study, Gillis and Carver (1980) failed to find support for the hypothesis that participants high in dispositional self-consciousness or with situationally elevated self-consciousness (as a result of exercising in front of a mirror) would show higher accuracy in estimating their heart rates after exercise.

Another series of studies examined whether traditional, instrument-based biofeedback training during exercise can help participants lower their physiological responses to exercise without reducing the amount of work being performed. In the first such study, Goldstein, Ross, and Brady (1977) found that five sessions of heart rate biofeedback training resulted in significant reductions in heart rate, systolic blood pressure, and rate–pressure product while walking on a treadmill. Furthermore, when the treatment was removed, the participants were able to maintain the reduced levels of heart rate, systolic blood pressure, and rate–pressure product. However, when the participants in the control group were subsequently introduced to biofeedback, they failed to show similar reductions.

Perski and Engel (1980) attempted to replicate the findings of this first study. They found that five heart rate biofeedback training sessions led to the experimental group having a heart rate that was significantly lower (by 15.2 beats/min or approximately 20%) compared to the control group during fixed-workload cycle ergometry exercise. Contrary to the findings of Goldstein et al. (1977), Perski and Engel found that, after the members of the control group underwent five sessions of biofeedback training, they were also able to significantly reduce their heart rate (by 13 beats/min). Finally, after the biofeedback treatment was removed for two sessions, the members of the experimental group were able to maintain the reduction in heart rate. On the other hand, biofeedback did not seem to have an effect on systolic blood pressure.

The exercise intensity used in Perski and Engel's (1980) study was approximately 50% of age-predicted maximal heart rate. In a follow-up study, Perski, Tzankoff, and Engel (1985) examined whether the findings could be replicated with a more vigorous exercise stimulus, namely 65% of maximal heart rate. After four training sessions during which they exercised while receiving heart rate biofeedback, the members of the experimental group showed an average heart rate elevation that was smaller by about 22% (12 beats/min) compared to the control group. On the other hand, there were no differences in systolic blood pressure. After the control participants underwent biofeedback training for four sessions, they also reduced their heart rates by about 9% (5 beats/min). Interestingly, additional analyses showed that the smaller heart rate elevations were not accompanied by compensatory physiological adjustments. There were no statistically significant differences in oxygen consumption, lactate accumulation, or indices of sympathetic nervous system activity (plasma epinephrine and norepinephrine concentrations). On the contrary, the lower heart rate was accompanied by lower pulmonary ventilation. Comparisons were also made during graded maximal tests performed before and after biofeedback training (the experimental group and the initial control group after biofeedback training were combined). In this case, both at a submaximal (75% of maximal heart rate) and at the maximal level, systolic blood pressure and rate-pressure product were lower after biofeedback training, but there were no significant changes in heart rate. Again, there were no signs of compensatory physiological adjustments, as there were no significant differences in ventilation, respiratory quotient, oxygen consumption, lactate accumulation, or epinephrine or norepinephrine concentration.

Studies by Lo and Johnston compared biofeedback to relaxation and also examined the role of instructions and habituation. In one study (Lo & Johnston, 1984a), an instructions-only condition, an inter-beat-interval (IBI) biofeedback condition, and a condition involving feedback on the product of IBI and pulse transit time (PTT) were compared. This product is almost perfectly negatively correlated with the rate–pressure product and is decreased with exercise. With respect to changes in IBI, four training sessions of IBI by PTT product biofeedback were significantly more effective than verbal instructions in increasing IBI (lowering heart rate). IBI-only biofeedback had intermediate effects and was associated with a gradual improvement across training sessions, but did not differ significantly from the other two conditions. The instructions-only condition was not associated with any changes. With respect to changes in PTT, both the IBI by PTT biofeedback condition and the IBI-only condition led to greater increases in the IBI by PTT product compared to instructions. Again, the instructions-only condition was not associated with any changes. The positive effects of biofeedback did not seem to transfer well, however, after the feedback was withdrawn. During a no-feedback fifth session, there were no differences between the conditions.

In another study, Lo and Johnston (1984b) compared the effects of IBI by PTT biofeedback to habituation (simply exercising) and Benson's relaxation response. Two exercise and two nonexercise training sessions were conducted. Compared to exercise before treatment, the biofeedback condition was associated with increases in IBI and was significantly different from both other conditions. With respect to PTT, the feedback condition was superior to habituation, whereas the relaxation condition was intermediate but did not differ significantly from the other two conditions. Only the feedback condition was associated with an improvement across trials. Finally, the frequency of respiration was slower in the feedback condition compared to the other two conditions.

Yamaji, Yokota, and Shephard (1992) conducted a case series study to examine the effects of using wrist-mounted heart rate monitors during track and cross-country training on the accuracy of heart rate estimations during different modes of exercise (treadmill, cycle ergometer, stair climber). Six runners wore heart rate monitors during their regular training (2 h/day, 3–4 days/week). Before and after a period of 13 weeks of training, they participated in multiple graded tests to exhaustion on a treadmill, a cycle ergometer, and a stair climber. The error of estimation (the discrepancy between perceptions of heart rate and ECG) improved in 6 of the 6 runners during treadmill running, in 4 of the 6 during cycle ergometry, but in only 2 of the 6 in stair climber exercise. After training, the regression lines of estimated and ECG-determined heart rate were closer to the line of identity in 6 of 6 treadmill tests, 5 of 6 cycle ergometer tests, and in 4 of 6 stair climber tests. In general, the discrepancies decreased with increasing exercise intensity.

Another study (Sada, Hamada, Yonezawa, & Ninomiya, 1999) examined the effects of a simple device designed to alert exercisers (with lights and sounds) when they exceeded a predetermined heart rate. Seven healthy males ran on a treadmill for five 6-min periods, while the target heart rate was set at 80, 100, 120, 140, and 160 beats/min, respectively. The participants overshot their target heart rates in 21 s when the target was 80 beats/min, in 40 s when the target was 120 beats/min and in 102 s when the target was 160 beats/min. Using the alarms, the participants adjusted their stride length and frequency and were able to keep their heart rates within 10% for a target heart rate of 80 beats/min, and within 4% for a target heart rate of 100–160 beats/min.

Two studies have examined the effects of noncardiovascular biofeedback. Kirkcaldy and Christen (1981) examined the effects of frontalis EMG biofeedback. They randomly assigned 26 male participants to one of four conditions: (a) frontalis EMG biofeedback during resting conditions (no exercise), (b) frontalis EMG biofeedback following exercise, (c) pseudo-feedback during resting conditions (no exercise), and (d) Jacobson's progressive relaxation during resting conditions (no exercise). Five training sessions were conducted. There were also five testing sessions, during which the participants performed one 8-min incremental bout of cycle ergometry (from 30 to 150 W). The first was a pretest, followed by a 15-min passive recovery. The second and third were interspersed with the training sessions and the fourth was a post-test. In these sessions, the first 10 min of post-exercise recovery were replaced by an application of the respective techniques. The fifth session was conducted seven weeks later, did not involve instrumentation, and its purpose was to test for retention. Only the group that received frontalis EMG biofeedback following exercise showed a reduction in frontalis muscle tension across sessions following exercise. At the post-test session, the mean EMG of the two biofeedback groups was significantly lower than the mean of the pseudo-feedback group, whereas the relaxation group showed a nonsignificant increase in tension. However, at the seven-week follow-up session, conducted without the benefit of biofeedback instrumentation, there were no signs of retention.

Hatfield, Spalding, Mahon, Slater, Brody, & Vaccaro (1992) examined the effects of providing biofeedback on the ventilatory equivalent for oxygen (V_E/VO_2) and the EMG activity of the trapezius muscle during running. A group of 12 male collegiate runners ran on a treadmill for three consecutive 12-min periods at an intensity that was just below their ventilatory threshold (71% $VO_{2_{max}}$). During one period, they received V_E/VO_2 and EMG biofeedback. During another period, their attention was distracted by means of a coincident timing task. Finally, one period did not involve a manipulation of the runners' attentional set and was used as a control. The results showed that V_E/VO_2, the ventilatory equivalent of carbon dioxide (V_E/VCO_2), ventilation, and respiratory rate were lower and tidal volume was higher during biofeedback than during the attentional distraction and control periods. Interestingly, despite the fact that ventilation was reduced during the biofeedback period, there were no differences in oxygen uptake between conditions, which suggests that there was a greater extraction of oxygen from inspired air per breath during biofeedback. Furthermore, the ratings of perceived exertion were lower during feedback and distraction compared to control. On the other hand, no effects on EMG were found.

The studies summarized up to this point all involved healthy participants. Positive effects, however, have also been found in cardiovascular patients. In an early uncontrolled case series study, Johnston and Lo (1983) examined 7 angina patients who underwent between 3 and 12 IBI by PTT biofeedback training sessions. All the patients were able to increase the IBI by PTT product while at rest but not during exercise. However, the frequency of chest pains was reduced in six of seven patients, the use of glycerine trinitrate (nitroglycerine) was reduced in all seven, and exercise tolerance during a Bruce protocol was improved in six of seven. In a subsequent study, Fredrikson and Engel (1985) examined 12 hypertensive patients. Half of them underwent five heart rate biofeedback training sessions. On average, their heart rate during exercise was approximately 9 beats/min lower than in control participants. Furthermore, although there were no differences in exercise workload, the biofeedback group showed lower oxygen consumption near the end of training. On the other hand, the groups did not differ in systolic blood pressure.

To date, there have been no extensive studies on the effects of biofeedback during strength training in humans. Johnston, Lo, Marie, and Van Jones (1982) briefly reported the results of a study comparing verbal instruction to decrease blood pressure to PTT biofeedback during 30 s of a 50% of maximal voluntary contraction with a hand grip dynamometer and a 60-s recovery period. Despite a tendency of the biofeedback condition to elicit longer IBIs and PTTs, the differences were not statistically significant. However, a series of studies in monkeys by Engel, Talan, and their associates suggests that a combination of heart rate biofeedback (a light indicating that heart rate was in the desired range) and operant conditioning (food reward and shock avoidance) can be effective in lowering heart rate and rate–pressure product while performing repeated weight lifts (see Engel & Talan, 1991a, for a review). The monkeys were trained to lift weights, to lower their heart rates, and finally to reliably combine these two skills (Engel & Talan, 1991b; Talan & Engel, 1986). The animals were able to attenuate the exercise-induced increases in heart rate in the combined condition while maintaining their cardiac output. This constitutes evidence of improved cardiac efficiency. Furthermore, the animals had lower respiratory quotient values during the combined condition (although this was due to greater oxygen uptake in two animals and lower carbon dioxide production in one animal). The attenuation of exercise-induced increases in heart rate was unaffected by α- and β-adrenergic and vagal blockades (Engel & Talan, 1991c), suggesting that the attenuation was not dependent on a specific autonomic reflex. Finally, Chefer, Talan, and Engel (1997) attempted to identify the brain centers that are responsible for the operant conditioning of heart rate by electrically stimulating 24 brain centers known to be involved in the regulation of heart rate (mainly thalamic and limbic nuclei) while the monkeys were performing the combined exercise–heart rate reduction task. Through this process, they identified a system (including the cingulate cortex, the mediodorsal nucleus, and the nucleus ventralis anterior) which increased heart rate when stimulated, but whose effect was significantly attenuated when the animals attempted to lower their heart rates. Chefer et al. expressed the belief that this system plays an important role in the central command of cardiovascular adaptations to exercise.

In summary, although the number of biofeedback studies that have been conducted in the context of exercise is not large and the methodological rigor of these studies varies widely, the results have been consistent. It appears that as few as four or five biofeedback training sessions may bring about a significant attenuation of exercise-induced increases in heart rate and rate–pressure product. It is also noteworthy that this effect appears to be the result of increases in the efficiency of cardiac function, as it cannot be explained by improvements in fitness, reductions in the amount of work performed, habituation to the experimental settings, or compensatory physiological adjustments. In other words, the benefits of biofeedback do not seem to be accompanied by any negative side effects. Furthermore, on the basis of the few studies conducted so far, it seems that biofeedback may be more effective for controlling cardiovascular responses during exercise than are verbal instructions or relaxation. On the other hand, there are other important questions that remain unanswered. The studies that used noncardiovascular channels as biofeedback sources are too few to allow for any definitive conclusions. Nevertheless, the study by Hatfield et al. (1992), in which biofeedback was based on the ventilatory equivalent for oxygen, produced some promising results. Even without having received training in using this parameter as biofeedback, the runners in the study were able to reduce several ventilatory parameters without reducing the amount of work being produced. Finally, much research is still needed to determine whether biofeedback can help regulate the physiological responses to weight training in humans. The pioneering studies by Engel and Talan (1991a) in monkeys suggest that this is possible.

THE PHENOMENOLOGY OF EXERCISE: BIOFEEDBACK WITHOUT INSTRUMENTS?

As noted previously, most biofeedback studies in the context of exercise have concentrated on heart rate as a biofeedback channel, in spite of the fact that without the benefit of instrumentation most people's ability to perceive their heart beats seems to remain modest even during exercise. However, decades of research on perceived exertion have demonstrated that there are a number of interoceptive cues (mainly associated with ventilation and muscular fatigue) that people can and do use in estimating their exertion levels during exercise (Sime, 1985). As we explained in a previous section, we are particularly interested in the transition from aerobic to anaerobic metabolism because this level of intensity appears to maximize the training benefits for previously untrained individuals without eliciting uniformly negative affective responses. From this perspective, it is noteworthy that the lactate and ventilatory thresholds, commonly used as indices of the aerobic–anaerobic transition, have been found to correspond to stable ratings of exertion that are generally unaffected by gender, training, or exercise modality (DeMello et al., 1987; Hetzler et al., 1991; Hill et al., 1987; Purvis & Cureton, 1981). In conjunction with the finding that exceeding the ventilatory threshold seems to be associated with an almost uniform decline in affective valence (Hall et al., 2002), these findings raise the possibility of using specific, individually determined ratings of perceived exertion and affective valence as targets for "interoceptive acuity" training, as a proxy to conventional, instrument-based biofeedback.

In the only known study to examine the effects of using feedback based on perceptions of exertion, Bayles et al. (1990) randomly assigned 30 participants to a practice-with-feedback group, a practice-without-feedback group, and a control group. Initially, all participants underwent a graded treadmill test. In a second session, each participant ran for 10 min at 40%, 60%, and 80% of their heart rate reserve in random order. During each trial, participants were "encouraged to internalize" their "subjective feelings" and "assign an overall perceptual rating to those sensations" (p. 27). During three subsequent trials, the participants were instructed to reproduce the exercise intensities "based on targeted perceptual ratings that they had assigned to the respective exercise intensities in trial 1" (p. 27). During a week between trials 2 and 3, the practice-with-feedback group and the practice-without-feedback group participated in a learning program which consisted of three periods. Also, during a week between trials 3 and 4, these groups participated in three exercise sessions on an indoor track at intensities that were individually selected to produce exertional sensations that were the same as those experienced during the treadmill exercise at 60% of heart rate reserve. Compared to the practice-without-feedback group, the practice-with-feedback group received taped reminders to think about (a) body temperature, (b) breathing, (c) comfort level, and (d) motivation. The main finding was that the practice-with-feedback group and the practice-without-feedback group both reduced their percent inaccuracy scores for running speed by 4.5% by trial 3 (averaged across the three intensities), whereas the control group increased their percent inaccuracy scores for running speed by 4.5%. For all three groups, the level of inaccuracy was maintained from trial 3 to trial 4. However, no effect on percent inaccuracy scores for heart rate or oxygen uptake was observed. Furthermore, it was found that the replication of heart rate and oxygen uptake values was more accurate at 60% and 80% of heart rate reserve compared to 40%.

Clearly, this area of research is in need of more information. Important questions that need to be addressed include (a) whether the combination of affect and exertion ratings can lead to improved self-regulation compared to methods based only on perceived exertion and (b) whether the relatively salient interoceptive cues that accompany the aerobic–anaerobic transition can serve as universal perceptual landmarks.

An important first step should be the systematic exploration of what has been called the "subjective symptomatology" or "phenomenology" of exercise (Dishman, 1994) and the aerobic–anaerobic transition, in particular. The present understanding of the subjective experiences that accompany exercise of various intensities remains very limited. In fact, not much progress has been made in this area since the pioneering studies by Kinsman and Weiser in the early 1970s (Kinsman & Weiser, 1976; Kinsman, Weiser, & Stamper, 1973; Weiser, Kinsman, & Stamper, 1973). This work was based on multivariate statistical methods (cluster and spherical analyses) that yield multidimensional representations of the relationships between perceived "symptoms" or cues associated with exercise. The results showed that the interoceptive and affective cues associated with exercise form distinct clusters, with each cluster contributing unique portions of the variance. However, this investigation was limited in several respects. First, it was based on a given list of items which may or may not adequately reflect the subjective experiences of diverse samples of exercise participants. Second, it was based on cycle ergometer exercise which emphasizes sensations localized in the legs and, thus, the results may not be generalizable to other modes of activity. Third, exercise intensity was based on an arbitrary percentage of maximal aerobic capacity and did not take into account the balance between aerobic and anaerobic metabolism. Fourth, no attempt was made to examine whether the emergent clusters could be used to differentiate between different levels of exercise intensity.

In spite of the limitations of this early research, it should be apparent that developing a better understanding of the subjective experiences associated with exercise, their verbal descriptors, and their dimensionality should improve communication between researchers and practitioners, as well as between practitioners and the public. The lack of this information is particularly noticeable in clinical applications of exercise. As one shocking example, there has never been a systematic exploration of the perceptual cues that can reliably distinguish between natural exertional symptoms and symptoms of exertional angina in cardiac patients. In the absence of this information, exercise practitioners have no basis upon which to educate patients on the cues that they can use to properly self-monitor and self-regulate the intensity of their physical activity.

FUTURE DIRECTIONS

Based on our review of this area of research, we propose the following. The first requisite step is an expansion of the current theoretical perspectives that consider the mind as the sole determinant of human experiences in the context of exercise. Instead, we advocate the development of integrative conceptual models that acknowledge the joint contributions of cognition and direct interoception in the process of generating subjective experiences in response to exercise.

Second, we believe that the research paradigm used in biofeedback studies in the context of exercise should be shifted from *visceral detection* to *visceral perception* (Pennebaker & Hoover, 1984). In other words, biofeedback training should incorporate perceived exertion and affective responses in addition to direct indices of physiological activity. Research suggests that, although it may be difficult for many individuals to accurately monitor isolated physiological parameters such as heart rate or blood pressure without extensive training, the accurate monitoring of the "gestalt" of exertional symptoms may be easier to achieve and, thus, more effective from a practical standpoint. In particular, the intensification of exertional symptoms and the negative shift in affective valence that accompany the transition to anaerobiosis may be used as "anchor points" to facilitate the training process.

Third, the study of the "subjective symptomatology" of exercise (Kinsman & Weiser, 1976; Kinsman et al., 1973; Weiser et al., 1973) must be revived and extended to a variety of exercise stimuli and populations, including patient populations with exercise-limiting conditions. The utility of this research should be obvious and its revival is long overdue.

Fourth, the utility of alternative physiological channels as sources of biofeedback should be explored. In addition to ventilatory parameters (Hatfield et al., 1992), it may be useful to examine the utility of blood lactate assessments. Although it remains impossible to assess blood lactate concentrations in real time, the advent of relatively inexpensive and simple-to-use portable lactate analyzers (Fell et al., 1998; Pyne et al., 2000) that yield results in 60 s creates some interesting possibilities. These analyzers may provide the easiest method of detecting the transition to anaerobic metabolism. The error grid technique used in the regulation of blood glucose in diabetics (Gonder-Frederick & Cox, 1991) could be adapted for the monitoring and regulation of lactate in the context of exercise. This simple technique involves plotting the estimated and assessed levels of lactate on a grid and noting the degree of deviation from the line of identity. Through the repeated use of the error grid and training in using pertinent sources of information, such as perceived exertion and affect, exercisers may improve their self-monitoring skills. The application of this method for the regulation of blood glucose has produced some promising results (Gonder-Frederick & Cox, 1991) that warrant attention.

For theoretical and practical reasons alike, biofeedback deserves more attention within exercise psychology than it has received until now. Undoubtedly, much work remains to be done. However, based on the positive findings that have accrued so far, it appears that biofeedback may be an effective method of improving the self-monitoring and self-regulation of exercise intensity in both healthy and clinical populations. By doing so, biofeedback may play a significant role in making exercise safer and more enjoyable and may, thus, contribute to the much-needed increase in the rates of adherence to exercise over the long haul.

CONCLUDING SUMMARY

The field of exercise psychology faces the great challenge of having to develop conceptual models to help understand exercise behavior and intervention methods for increasing exercise participation and long-term adherence. One mechanism that is likely to influence exercise behavior but has received relatively little attention is one in which a critical role is attributed to the intensity of exercise and its effects on the quality of the experience that participants derive from their involvement. On the one hand, if the intensity of exercise is too low, the possibility of substantial health and fitness benefits is reduced, increasing the likelihood of dropout due to frustration stemming from unfulfilled expectations. On the other hand, if the intensity of exercise is too high (according to accumulating evidence, if it exceeds the point of transition from aerobic to anaerobic metabolism), most individuals report feeling progressively worse and rate the intensity as "hard." Over time, such unpleasant experiences may lead to an aversion to exercise, again raising the possibility of dropout. The conclusion that emerges is that accurate self-monitoring and self-regulation of exercise intensity could have a significant impact on subsequent exercise behavior by influencing the quality of the experience that individuals derive from exercise.

In this context, biofeedback can prove to be a powerful tool for teaching exercisers to maintain the delicate balance between exercise intensity that is effective on the one hand and pleasant or tolerable and safe on the other. The studies on the effects of biofeedback in the context of exercise are few, but have consistently demonstrated that even as little as four or five sessions of biofeedback training can attenuate the exercise-induced increases in physiological activation without reducing the amount of work being performed. From an applied standpoint, it is also important that these effects seem to be the results of improved efficiency in physiological function, as there have been no indications of negative side effects, such as compensatory physiological adjustments. Although the extant evidence supports the use of biofeedback in practice, research should continue and its scope should be expanded, placing emphasis on the use of noncardiovascular (e.g., ventilatory, blood lactate, etc.) biofeedback modes, the linkage of biofeedback to exertional and affective experiences, and the investigation of the content, the verbal descriptors, and the dimensionality of such experiences.

REFERENCES

Acevedo, E. O., Rinehardt, K. F., & Kraemer, R. R. (1994). Perceived exertion and affect at varying intensities of running. *Research Quarterly for Exercise and Sport*, **65**, 372–376.

American College of Sports Medicine (2000). *ACSM guidelines for exercise testing and prescription* (6th ed.). Baltimore, MD: Williams & Wilkins.

Averill, J. R. (1980). A constructivist view of emotion. In R. Plutchik & H. Kellerman (eds.), *Emotion: Theory, research, and experience* (vol. 1; pp. 305–339). New York: Academic.

Bandura, A. (1982). Self-efficacy mechanism in human agency. *American Psychologist*, **37**, 122–147.

Bayles, C. M., Metz, K. F., Robertson, R., Goss, F. L., Cosgrove, J., & McBurney, D. (1990). Perceptual regulation of prescribed exercise. *Journal of Cardiopulmonary Rehabilitation*, **10**, 25–31.

Belman, M. J., & Gaesser, G. A. (1991). Exercise training below and above the lactate threshold in the elderly. *Medicine and Science in Sports and Exercise*, **23**, 562–568.

Borg, G., Ljunggren, G., & Ceci, R. (1985). The increase of perceived exertion, aches and pain in the legs, heart rate and blood lactate during exercise on a bicycle ergometer. *European Journal of Applied Physiology*, **54**, 343–349.

Boutcher, S. H., & Trenske, M. (1990). The effects of sensory deprivation and music on perceived exertion and affect during exercise. *Journal of Sport & Exercise Psychology*, **12**, 167–176.

Brewer, B. W., Manos, T. M., McDevitt, A. V., Cornelius, A. E., & Van Raalte, J. L. (2000). The effect of adding lower intensity work on perceived aversiveness of exercise. *Journal of Sport & Exercise Psychology*, **22**, 119–130.

Brownell, K. D. (1991). Personal responsibility and control over our bodies: When expectation exceeds reality. *Health Psychology*, **10**, 303–310.

Brubaker, P. H., Rejeski, W. J., Law, H. C., Pollock, W. H., Wurst, M. E., & Miller, H. S. (1994). Cardiac patients' perception of work intensity during graded exercise testing: Do they generalize to field settings? *Journal of Cardiopulmonary Rehabilitation*, **14**, 127–133.

Chefer, S. I., Talan, M. I., & Engel, B. T. (1997). Central neural correlates of learned heart rate control during exercise: Central command demystified. *Journal of Applied Physiology*, **83**, 1448–1453.

Chow, R. J., & Wilmore, J. H. (1984). The regulation of exercise intensity by ratings of perceived exertion. *Journal of Cardiac Rehabilitation*, **4**, 382–387.

DeMello, J. J., Cureton, K. J., Boineau, R. E., & Singh, M. M. (1987). Ratings of perceived exertion at the lactate threshold in trained and untrained men and women. *Medicine and Science in Sports and Exercise*, **19**, 354–362.

Desharnais, R., Bouillon, J., & Godin, G. (1986). Participants' early impressions of a supervised exercise program as a determinant of their subsequent adherence. *Perceptual and Motor Skills*, **64**, 847–850.

Dishman, R. K. (1994). Prescribing exercise intensity for healthy adults using perceived exertion. *Medicine and Science in Sports and Exercise*, **26**, 1087–1094.

Dishman, R. K., & Buckworth, J. (1996). Increasing physical activity: A quantitative synthesis. *Medicine and Science in Sports and Exercise*, **28**, 706–719.

Dwyer, J., & Bybee, R. (1983). Heart rate indices of the anaerobic threshold. *Medicine and Science in Sports and Exercise*, **15**, 72–76.

Ekkekakis, P., & Petruzzello, S. J. (1999). Acute aerobic exercise and affect: Current status, problems, and prospects regarding dose-response. *Sports Medicine*, **28**, 337–374.

Emmons, R. A., & Diener, E. (1986). A goal-affect analysis of everyday situational choices. *Journal of Research in Personality*, **20**, 309–326.

Engel, B. T., & Talan, M. I. (1991a). Cardiovascular responses as behavior. *Circulation*, **83** [Supplement II], 9–13.

Engel, B. T., & Talan, M. I. (1991b). Hemodynamic and respiratory concomitants of learned heart rate control during exercise. *Psychophysiology*, **28**, 225–230.

Engel, B. T., & Talan, M. I. (1991c). Autonomic blockade does not prevent learned heart rate attenuation during exercise. *Physiology and Behavior*, **49**, 373–382.

Epstein, L. H., Koeske, R., & Wing, R. R. (1984). Adherence to exercise in obese children. *Journal of Cardiac Rehabilitation*, **4**, 185–195.

Eston, R. G., Davies, B. L., & Williams, J. G. (1987). Use of perceived effort ratings to control exercise intensity in young healthy adults. *European Journal of Applied Physiology*, **56**, 222–224.

Eston, R. G., & Williams, J. G. (1988). Reliability of ratings of perceived effort regulation of exercise intensity. *British Journal of Sports Medicine*, **22**, 153–155.

Fell, J. W., Rayfield, J. M., Gulbin, J. P., & Gaffney, P. T. (1998). Evaluation of the Accusport lactate analyser. *International Journal of Sports Medicine*, **19**, 199–204.

Fredrikson, M., & Engel, B. T. (1985). Learned control of heart rate during exercise in patients with borderline hypertension. *European Journal of Applied Physiology*, **54**, 315–320.

Gillis, R., & Carver, C. S. (1980). Self-focus and estimation of heart rate following physical exertion. *Bulletin of the Psychonomic Society*, **15**, 118–120.

Gilman, M. B., & Wells, C. L. (1993). The use of heart rates to monitor exercise intensity in relation to metabolic variables. *International Journal of Sports Medicine*, **14**, 339–344.

Goldstein, D. S., Ross, R. S., & Brady, J. V. (1977). Biofeedback heart rate training during exercise. *Biofeedback and Self-Regulation*, **2**, 107–125.

Gonder-Frederick, L. A., & Cox, D. J. (1991). Symptom perception, symptom beliefs, and blood glucose discrimination in the self-treatment of insulin-dependent diabetes. In J. A. Skelton & R. T. Croyle (eds.), *Mental representation in health and illness* (pp. 220–246). New York: Springer-Verlag.

Green, J. M., Michael, T., & Solomon, A. H. (1999). The validity of ratings of perceived exertion for cross-modal regulation of swimming intensity. *Journal of Sports Medicine and Physical Fitness*, **39**, 207–212.

Gutmann, M. C., Squires, R. W., Pollock, M. L., Foster, C., & Anholm, J. (1981). Perceived exertion—heart rate relationship during exercise testing and training in cardiac patients. *Journal of Cardiac Rehabilitation*, **1**, 52–59.

Hall, E. E., Ekkekakis, P., & Petruzzello, S. J. (2002). The affective beneficence of vigorous exercise revisited. *British Journal of Health Psychology*, *7*, 47–66.

Hardy, C. J., & Rejeski, W. J. (1989). Not what, but how one feels: The measurement of affect during exercise. *Journal of Sport & Exercise Psychology*, **11**, 304–317.

Hardy, C. S., Hall, E. G., & Prestholdt, P. H. (1986). The mediational role of social influence in the perception of exertion. *Journal of Sport Psychology*, **8**, 88–104.

Hatfield, B. D., Spalding, T. W., Mahon, A. D., Slater, B. A., Brody, E. B., & Vaccaro, P. (1992). The effect of psychological strategies upon cardiorespiratory and muscular activity during treadmill running. *Medicine and Science in Sports and Exercise*, **24**, 218–225.

Hetzler, R. K., Seip, R. L., Boutcher, S. H., Pierce, E., Snead, D., & Weltman, A. (1991). Effect of exercise modality on ratings of perceived exertion at various lactate concentrations. *Medicine and Science in Sports and Exercise*, **23**, 88–92.

Hill, D. W., Cureton, K. J., Grisham, S. C., & Collins, M. A. (1987). Effect of training on the rating of perceived exertion at the ventilatory threshold. *European Journal of Applied Physiology*, **56**, 206–211.

Hodes, R. L., Howland, E. W., Lightfoot, N., & Cleeland, C. S. (1990). The effects of distraction on responses to cold pressor pain. *Pain*, **41**, 109–114.

Hollandsworth, J. G. (1979). Some thoughts on distance running as training in biofeedback. *Journal of Sport Behavior*, **2**, 71–82.

Hollandsworth, J. G., & Jones, G. E. (1979). Perceptions of arousal and awareness of physiological responding prior to and after running 20 kilometers. *Journal of Sport Psychology*, **1**, 291–300.

Jacobsen, S., & Johansen, O. (1974). An ergometer bicycle controlled by heart rate. *Medical and Biological Engineering*, **12**, 675–680.

Johnston, D. W., & Lo, C. R. (1983). The effects of cardiovascular feedback and relaxation on angina pectoris. *Behavioural Psychotherapy*, **11**, 257–264.

Johnston, D. W., Lo, C. R., Marie, G. V., & Van Jones, J. (1982). Self-control of inter-beat interval and pulse transit time at rest and during exercise: A preliminary report. *Acta Medica Scandinavica Supplementum*, **660**, 238–243.

Jones, G. E. (1994). Perception of visceral sensations: A review of recent findings, methodologies, and future directions. In J. R. Jennings, P. K. Ackles, & M. G. H. Coles (eds.), *Advances in psychophysiology: A research annual* (vol. **5**; pp. 55–191). London: Jessica Kingsley.

Jones, G. E., & Hollandsworth, J. G. (1981). Heart rate discrimination before and after exercise-induced augmented cardiac activity. *Psychophysiology*, **18**, 252–257.

Katch, V., Weltman, A., Sady, S., & Freedson, P. (1978). Validity of the relative percent concept for equating training intensity. *European Journal of Applied Physiology*, **39**, 219–227.

Kawada, T., Sunagawa, G., Takaki, H., Shishido, T., Miyano, H., Miyashita, H., Sato, T., Sugimachi, M., & Sunagawa, K. (1999). Development of a servo-controller of heart rate using a treadmill. *Japanese Circulation Journal*, **63**, 945–950.

Kinsman, R. A., & Weiser, P. C. (1976). Subjective symptomatology during work and fatigue. In E. Simonson & P. C. Weiser (eds.), *Psychological aspects and physiological correlates of work and fatigue* (pp. 336–405). Springfield, IL: Charles C. Thomas.

Kinsman, R. A., Weiser, P. C., & Stamper, D. A. (1973). Multidimensional analysis of subjective symptomatology during prolonged strenuous exercise. *Ergonomics*, **16**, 211–226.

Kirkcaldy, B. D., & Christen, J. (1981). An investigation into the effect of EMG frontalis biofeedback on physiological correlates of exercise. *International Journal of Sport Psychology*, **12**, 235–252.

Kollenbaum, V. E. (1994). A clinical method for the assessment of interoception of cardiovascular strain in CHD patients. *Journal of Psychophysiology*, **8**, 121–130.

Kollenbaum, V. E., Dahme, B., & Kirchner, G. (1996). "Interoception" of heart rate, blood pressure, and myocardial metabolism during ergometric work load in healthy young subjects. *Biological Psychology*, **42**, 183–197.

Kosiek, R. M., Szymanski, L. M., Lox, C. L., Kelley, G., & MacFarlane, P. A. (1999). Self-regulation of exercise intensity in cardiac rehabilitation patients. *Sports Medicine Training and Rehabilitation*, **8**, 359–368.

Laperriere, A. R., VanDercar, D. H., Shyu, L. Y., Ward, M. F., McCabe, P. M., Perry, A. C., Mosher, P. E., & Schneiderman, N. (1989). Microcomputer servo-controlled bicycle ergometer system for psychophysiological research. *Psychophysiology*, **26**, 201–207.

Lazarus, R. S. (1975). A cognitively oriented psychologist looks at biofeedback. *American Psychologist*, **30**, 553–561.

Lazarus, R. S. (1977). A cognitive analysis of biofeedback control. In G. E. Schwartz & J. Beatty (eds.), *Biofeedback: Theory and Research* (pp. 67–87). New York: Academic.

Lazarus, R. S. (1991). Progress on a cognitive-motivational-relational theory of emotion. *American Psychologist*, **46**, 819–834.

Lee, C. (1995). Comparing the incommensurable: Where science and politics collide. *Journal of Behavior Therapy and Experimental Psychiatry*, **26**, 259–263.

Lee, I. M., Hsieh, C. C., & Paffenbarger, R. S. Jr. (1995). Exercise intensity and longevity in men: the Harvard Alumni Health Study. *Journal of the American Medical Association*, **273**, 1179–1184.

Lee, J. Y., Jensen, B. E., Oberman, A., Fletcher, G. F., Fletcher, B. J., & Raczynski, J. M. (1996). Adherence in the Training Levels Comparison Trial. *Medicine and Science in Sports and Exercise*, **28**, 47–52.

Lo, C. R., & Johnston, D. W. (1984a). Cardiovascular feedback during dynamic exercise. *Psychophysiology*, **21**, 199–206.

Lo, C. R., & Johnston, D. W. (1984b). The self-control of the cardiovascular response to exercise using feedback of the product of interbeat interval and pulse transit time. *Psychosomatic Medicine*, **46**, 115–125.

McAuley, E. (1994). Enhancing psychological health through physical activity. In H. A. Quinney, L. Gauvin, & A. E. T. Wall (eds.), *Toward active living: Proceedings of the international conference on physical activity, fitness, and health* (pp. 83–90). Champaign, IL: Human Kinetics.

Montgomery, W. A., Jones, G. E., & Hollandsworth, J. G. (1984). The effects of physical fitness and exercise on cardiac awareness. *Biological Psychology*, **18**, 11–22.

Morgan, W. P. (1989). Sport psychology in its own context: A recommendation for the future. In J. S. Skinner & C. B. Corbin (eds.), *Future directions in exercise and sport science research* (pp. 97–110). Champaign, IL: Human Kinetics.

Morris, J. N. (1996). Exercise versus heart attack: questioning the consensus? *Research Quarterly for Exercise and Sport*, **67**, 216–220.

National Institutes of Health (1996). NIH consensus development panel on physical activity and cardiovascular health: Physical activity and cardiovascular health. *Journal of the American Medical Association*, **276**, 241–246.

Noble, B. J., & Robertson, R. J. (1996). *Perceived exertion*. Champaign, IL: Human Kinetics.

Parfitt, G., & Eston, R. (1995). Changes in ratings of perceived exertion and psychological affect in the early stages of exercise. *Perceptual and Motor Skills*, **80**, 259–266.

Parfitt, G., Eston, R., & Connolly, D. (1996). Psychological affect at different ratings of perceived exertion in high-and low-active women: A study using a production protocol. *Perceptual and Motor Skills*, **82**, 1035–1042.

Parfitt, G., Markland, D., & Holmes, C. (1994). Responses to physical exertion in active and inactive males and females. *Journal of Sport & Exercise Psychology*, **16**, 178–186.

Pennebaker, J. W., & Hoover, C. W. (1984). Visceral perception and visceral detection: Disentangling methods and assumptions. *Biofeedback and Self-Regulation*, **9**, 339–352.

Perski, A., & Engel, B. T. (1980). The role of behavioral conditioning in the cardiovascular adjustment to exercise. *Biofeedback and Self-Regulation*, **5**, 91–104.

Perski, A., Tzankoff, S. P., & Engel, B. T. (1985). Central control of cardiovascular adjustments to exercise. *Journal of Applied Physiology*, **58**, 431–435.

Petruzzello, S. J., Landers, D. M., & Salazar, W. (1991). Biofeedback and sport/exercise performance: Applications and limitations. *Behavior Therapy*, **22**, 379–392.

Potteiger, J. A., & Evans, B. W. (1995). Using heart rate and ratings of perceived exertion to monitor intensity in runners. *Journal of Sports Medicine and Physical Fitness*, **35**, 181–186.

Pratt, W. M., Siconolfi, S. F., Webster, L., Hayes, J. C., Mazzocca, A. D., & Harris, B. A. (1991). A comparison between computer-controlled and set work rate exercise based on target heart rate. *Aviation, Space, and Environmental Medicine*, **62**, 899–902.

Purvis, J. W., & Cureton, K. J. (1981). Ratings of perceived exertion at the anaerobic threshold. *Ergonomics*, **24**, 295–300.

Pyne, D. B., Boston, T., Martin, D. T., & Logan, A. (2000). Evaluation of the Lactate Pro blood lactate analyzer. *European Journal of Applied Physiology*, **82**, 112–116.

Rejeski, W. J. (1981). The perception of exertion: A social psychophysiological integration. *Journal of Sport Psychology*, **4**, 305–320.

Rejeski, W. J. (1985). Perceived exertion: An active or passive process. *Journal of Sport Psychology*, **7**, 371–378.

Rejeski, W. J., & Ribisl, P. M. (1980). Expected task duration and perceived effort: An attributional analysis. *Journal of Sport Psychology*, **2**, 227–236.

Rejeski, W. J., & Thompson, A. (1993). Historical and conceptual roots of exercise psychology. In P. Seraganian (ed.), *Exercise psychology: The influence of physical exercise on psychological processes* (pp. 3–35). New York: John Wiley.

Robertson, R.J. (1982). Central signals of perceived exertion during dynamic exercise. *Medicine and Science in Sports and Exercise*, **14**, 390–396.

Sada, K., Hamada, S., Yonezawa, Y., & Ninomiya, I. (1999). Self-biofeedback control of heart rate during exercise. *Japanese Journal of Physiology*, **49**, 275–281.

Sallis, J. F., Haskell, W. L., Fortmann, S. P., Vranizan, K. M., Taylor, C. B., & Solomon, D. S. (1986). Predictors of adoption and maintenance of physical activity in a community sample. *Preventive Medicine*, **15**, 331–341.

Sime, W. E. (1985). Physiological perception: The key to peak performance in athletic competition. In J. H. Sandweiss & S. L. Wolf (eds.), *Biofeedback and sports science* (pp. 33–62). New York: Plenum.

Smutok, M. A., Skrinar, G. S., & Pandolf, K. B. (1980). Exercise intensity: Regulation by perceived exertion. *Archives of Physical Medicine and Rehabilitation*, **61**, 569–574.

Talan, M. I., & Engel, B. T. (1986). Learned control of heart rate during dynamic exercise in nonhuman primates. *Journal of Applied Physiology*, **61**, 545–553.

Thompson, D. L., & West, K. A. (1998). Ratings of perceived exertion to determine intensity during outdoor running. *Canadian Journal of Applied Physiology*, **23**, 56–65.

United States Department of Health and Human Services (1996). *Physical activity and health: A report of the Surgeon General.* Atlanta, GA: U.S. Department of Health and Human Services, Centers for Disease Control and Prevention, National Center for Chronic Disease Prevention and Health Promotion.

United States Department of Health and Human Services. (2000). *Healthy people 2010.* Washington, DC: Author.

United States National Center for Health Statistics (1999). *Healthy people 2000 review, 1998–1999.* Hyattsville, MD: Public Health Service.

Weiser, P. C., Kinsman, R. A., & Stamper, D. A. (1973). Task-specific symptomatology changes resulting from prolonged submaximal bicycle riding. *Medicine and Science in Sports*, **5**, 79– 85.

Weltman, A., Seip, R. L., Snead, D., Weltman, J. Y., Haskvitz, E. M., Evans, W. S., Veldhuis, J. D., & Rogol, A. D. (1992). Exercise training at and above the lactate threshold in previously untrained women. *International Journal of Sports Medicine*, **13**, 257–263.

Whaley, M. H., & Forsyth, G. (1990). The value of traditional intensity feedback for self-regulation of initial exercise training. *Journal of Cardiopulmonary Rehabilitation*, **10**, 98–106.

Whaley, M. H., Woodall, M. T., Kaminsky, L. A., & Emmett, J. D. (1997). Reliability of perceived exertion during graded exercise testing in apparently healthy adults. *Journal of Cardiopulmonary Rehabilitation*, **17**, 37–42.

Winett, R. A. (1998). Developing more effective health-behavior programs: Analyzing the epidemiological and biological bases for activity and exercise programs. *Applied & Preventive Psychology*, **7**, 209–224.

Yamaji, K., Yokota, Y., & Shephard, R. J. (1992). A comparison of the perceived and the ECG measured heart rate during cycle ergometer, treadmill and stairmill exercise before and after perceived heart rate training. *Journal of Sports Medicine and Physical Fitness*, **32**, 271–281.

Zaichkowsky, L. D., & Fuchs, C. Z. (1988). Biofeedback applications in exercise and athletic performance. *Exercise and Sport Sciences Reviews*, **16**, 381–421.

CHAPTER 6

Biofeedback: Applications and Methodological Concerns

Gershon Tenenbaum, Mandy Corbett, and Anastasia Kitsantas

INTRODUCTION

Biofeedback and biofeedback training are aimed at assisting individuals to gain voluntary control over the various psychophysiological processes that had been previously considered to be "involuntary" and beyond conscious awareness. The literature reveals that biofeedback has been extensively used in both clinical and sport settings; however, the research over the years has failed to produce conclusive evidence that biofeedback is an effective technique for assisting individuals to gain such self-regulatory control. Yet it is not possible to conclude that biofeedback as a technique has in fact failed, because unexpected findings may be attributed to inherent flaws in the methodology employed rather than to the biofeedback technique itself (Ancoli & Kamiya, 1978). As highlighted by Yates (1980), empirical knowledge is a function of the methodology used to generate that knowledge, and significant changes in empirical knowledge very often result from important changes in methodology. Thus, a need exists to look beyond the results of biofeedback studies and spend more time interpreting what the findings of those studies mean in light of the methodology employed.

Taking into consideration the argument above, it is the intention of this chapter to alert the reader to the methodological concerns evident in various studies that have ultimately led researchers and practitioners to question the efficacy of biofeedback as a technique to aid in self-regulation. The chapter begins with clarifying and differentiating the terms "biofeedback" and "biofeedback training." Thereafter, a brief description of the most commonly employed biofeedback modalities are presented, and the methodological concerns that are evident in both biofeedback research and practice, particularly in the area of sport and exercise, are pointed out. Next, taking into account the methodological concerns, recommendations are made on how instructors

Brain and Body in Sport and Exercise: Biofeedback Applications in Performance Enhancement.
Edited by Boris Blumenstein, Michael Bar-Eli, and Gershon Tenenbaum.

can teach athletes to incorporate biofeedback into their daily practice routines via self-regulation strategies on their own in order to maximize performance. Finally, conclusions and suggestions for future research are presented.

WHAT IS BIOFEEDBACK AND BIOFEEDBACK TRAINING?

Originating out of earlier research pertaining to animal and human learning, biofeedback, as a term and as an area of inquiry and application, began appearing in the literature in the 1960s (Fischer-Williams, Nigl, & Sovine, 1981; Zaichkowsky & Fuchs, 1988). The primary aim of biofeedback training as a technique to be employed in various applied settings was, and still is, to facilitate the learning of self-regulation of various physiological arousal states. Although the terms "biofeedback" and "biofeedback training" are frequently used synonymously (the term "biofeedback" incorrectly used to refer to biofeedback training), they are not in fact synonymous and thus need to be differentiated.

Biofeedback involves the use of some type of instrumentation (usually an electronic device with sensors and transducers) in order to detect and monitor particular biological responses that the individual is not normally aware of or able to control voluntarily, for example, heart rate, muscle tension, skin temperature and brain wave activity (Ash & Zellner, 1978; Fischer-Williams et al., 1981; Heil & Henschen, 1996; Zaichkowsky & Fuchs, 1989). Once the meaningful biological information is precisely detected it is then amplified and rapidly "fed back" to the individual; hence the term "biofeedback" (Zaichkowsky & Takenaka, 1993). The biofeedback information is usually in the form of a numerical, auditory, or visual feedback signal (Zaichkowsky & Fuchs, 1988, 1989). Whilst the term "biofeedback" is still used, the physiological information reflecting the underlying biological functions has more recently been referred to as psychophysiological information, since physiological processes have been shown to be influenced by psychological responses (Amar, 1993; Fischer-Williams et al., 1981; Shellenberger & Green, 1986). The advent of psychophysiology has brought with it a fusion of the psyche and soma duality in a way that had previously not often been attained.

Along with the development of instruments aimed at measuring the underlying physiological responses, researchers began to question whether or not those physiological responses that were considered to be involuntary could in fact be consciously controlled (Miller, 1969). This lead to what is referred to as *biofeedback training*.

Biofeedback training is a technique that goes one step beyond merely referring to the biofeedback (or psychophysiological) information that provides one with some awareness of particular autonomic responses. Biofeedback training actively involves the individual using the biofeedback information so as to gain voluntary control over the "involuntary" psychophysiological processes concerned (Hackfort & Schwenkmezger, 1993; Zaichkowsky & Fuchs, 1988, 1989). Whilst biofeedback training has been used extensively in the treatment of health-related disorders such as hypertension, tension headaches, migraine headaches, anxiety disorders, Raynaud's disease, and insomnia (see Collins, 1995; Shellenberger & Green, 1986), biofeedback training has also been used in performance-related areas (Petruzzello, Landers, & Salazar, 1991).

With reference to sport settings, particularly where elite athletes are involved, biofeedback training seems, at least at face value, to be highly appropriate since the measurement of autonomic responses by psychophysiological assessment seems especially relevant because of the psychological stressors inherent in such a competitive environment. Furthermore, athletes are accustomed and motivated to continuously evaluate their performance and thereby take feedback into account (Blumenstein, Bar-Eli, & Tenenbaum, 1997).

Research on, and application of, biofeedback training in the exercise and sport sciences first appeared in the mid 1970s (Zaichkowsky, 1975). Since then, many investigations have taken place and the accumulation of data has been impressive (Fischer-Williams et al., 1981). Although findings have at times appeared controversial, the potential that biofeedback training has for the understanding and enhancement of athletic performance has been recognised (see Collins, 1995; Petruzzello et al., 1991; Sandweiss & Wolf, 1985; Zaichkowsky & Fuchs, 1988, 1989). In sport, whilst most research has focused on evaluating the efficacy of biofeedback training in helping athletes lower their arousal, stress, and performance anxiety levels (De Witt, 1980; Murphy & Woolfolk, 1987), other studies have examined the use of biofeedback training to increase muscle strength, reduce pain and fatigue, increase flexibility, and regulate heart rate (Blumenstein et al., 1997). The major modalities that have been utilized in sport and exercise settings to aid biofeedback training are briefly outlined below (note that these are elaborated in more detail in other chapters in this book).

Muscle feedback. An electromyograph (EMG) is used to detect and measure muscle activity. Once detected, the electrical activity of the target muscle, or muscles, is displayed (fed back) to the individual. The individual then tries to modify the EMG signal in the appropriate direction by relaxing tense muscles or activating muscles that are injured and/or partially paralyzed (Wolf, 1983; Zaichkowsky & Fuchs, 1988, 1989).

Thermal biofeedback. Thermal biofeedback primarily involves the use of skin temperature of the fingers to indirectly measure the sympathetic arousal of the autonomic nervous system (Zaichkowsky & Fuchs, 1989). People who are in a stressful situation often experience a sense of coldness in their hands, the reason being that when one is stressed, tense, or anxious, the smooth muscles surrounding the blood vessels contract, thereby decreasing peripheral blood flow, which results in lowered skin temperature. Conversely, when one is calm and relaxed, an increase in the temperature of the extremities is detected (Fischer-Williams et al., 1981)

Electrodermal biofeedback. Feedback obtained from electrical activity at various skin sites is referred to as Electrodermal biofeedback. Specific measures of electrodermal feedback include galvanic skin response (GSR), skin conductance response (SCR), skin resistance response (SRR), skin conductance level (SCL), skin resistance level (SRL), and skin potential response (SPR). Electrodermal biofeedback has mainly been used as an adjunct in teaching relaxation, often in combination with thermal regulation (Zaichkowsky & Fuchs, 1988, 1989). Although electrodermal biofeedback has also been used in an attempt to reduce precompetition and competition anxiety, changes in performance have not been found to be a direct result of this biofeedback training intervention (Zaichkowsky & Fuchs, 1988).

Cardiovascular biofeedback. Cardiovascular biofeedback has been used by researchers and clinicians to provide feedback about heart rate and blood flow (Zaichkowsky & Fuchs, 1989). In the clinical domain, cardiovascular biofeedback has been implemented as a means of overcoming cardiac arrhythmias, hypertension, and vasoconstrictive disorders (e.g., Engle & Bailey, 1983) whereas in sport and exercise it has been associated with better golf putting performance (Boutcher & Zinsser, 1990) and significant improvements in both shooting performance and coordination of the motor act of firing (Daniels & Landers, 1981).

Electroencephalographic biofeedback. Electroencephalographic (EEG) biofeedback involves the measurement of brainwave activity. EEG activity is recorded at the scalp and can be broken down into numerous bandwidths based on frequency components. The most frequently used bandwidth in biofeedback investigations appears to be the alpha bandwidth (8–12 Hz) (Petruzzello et al., 1991). According to Kamiya (1968) and Nowlis and Kamiya (1970), people can learn to alter their brainwave activity such that the duration of alpha activity dominance can be increased to some extent. It has been claimed that when alpha waves predominate, people are in their most creative state, are at their highest level of inspiration, experience enhanced memory, concentration, and learning, and tend to express better decision-making abilities (Heibloem, 1990).

METHODOLOGICAL CONCERNS

Although most research pertaining to biofeedback (in both clinical and sport settings) took place in the late 1970s and the 1980s, the modification of athletes' arousal states using various biofeedback instruments continues to be of great interest to coaches, athletes, and applied sport psychologists (Collins, 1995; Zaichkowsky & Takenaka, 1993). There are, however, numerous methodological issues evident in past research, in both the clinical and sporting domains, that need to be highlighted, the most noteworthy of which are presented next. It is not the focus of this chapter to highlight the methodological concerns specific to any one particular modality or setting. Rather, the focus is on common methodological issues that need be considered by all biofeedback researchers, clinicians, and practitioners, regardless of the modalities involved or the context of the setting. Whilst many of the methodological concerns are in fact interrelated, they are presented separately in Table 6.1 for purposes of simplicity and are discussed extensively below.

Table 6.1 Methodological concerns of research conducted on biofeedback

1. Frequency and length of training sessions
2. Training criteria
3. Homework sessions
4. Internal locus of control
5. Motivation
6. Cognitive support
7. Significant others and social facilitation
8. Relaxation–biofeedback comparison groups
9. Baseline readings
10. Statistical versus clinical significance
11. Adaptation
12. Multifaceted treatment programs

Frequency and Length of Training Sessions

A large number of biofeedback studies in the clinical area that have used a minimal number of training sessions and/or training sessions of insufficient duration have produced unsuccessful results (Shellenberger & Green, 1986). Having reviewed over 300 studies pertaining to biofeedback training, Shellenberger and Green concluded that many training sessions documented in the research literature are less than 20 min in length and some even less than 3 min. Ancoli and Kamiya (1978) reported a similar finding. With reference to alpha biofeedback training sessions, Ancoli and Kamiya noted that trial lengths reported in some of the research were as short as 2 min in length—a duration far too short for effective training.

According to Shellenberger and Green (1986), conducting biofeedback training for an insufficient duration or over an insufficient number of training sessions could stem from the misconception that biofeedback is a treatment, like a drug, rather than a tool. Biofeedback is not a treatment that has specific drug-like effects. Rather, biofeedback is merely the emission of information, via appropriate instruments, about ongoing changes in some biological functions. These instruments do not have inherent powers to create, control, or even change behavior; they simply reflect it. Biofeedback as a training technique is, as stated earlier in this volume, an educational process through which the individual learns to recognize physiological responses as presented by biofeedback equipment (the tool) and consciously has to learn to alter the responses via biofeedback training and self-regulation. Learning, as opposed to simply obtaining the biofeedback information, is the critical phenomenon (Rosenfeld, 1987; Shellenberger & Green, 1986). Like all types of learning, in order to be effective, biofeedback training requires systematic practice of sufficient length and duration combined with some form of feedback information (Ancoli & Kamiya, 1978; Zaichkowsky & Fuchs, 1988). The use of an insufficient number of training sessions is like attempting to train a rifle shooter in just one session to decrease his/her heart rate from 70 beats to 60 beats per minute and fail, then concluding that humans are unable to control their heart beat and furthermore that the heart rate monitor is not useful.

Linked to the concern regarding both the frequency and duration of training sessions is the issue of training criteria.

Training Criteria

The failure to establish training criteria and to train subjects accordingly has resulted in a failure to appreciate and understand the essential link between training and the treatment effect or degree of symptom alteration (Blanchard, Adrasik & Silver, 1980; Steiner & Dince, 1981, 1983). As already mentioned, biofeedback is not a treatment; it has no specific effects. Rather, self-regulation is learned through training with the use of biofeedback information, and the resultant effect is psychophysiological self-regulation (Shellenberger & Green, 1987). Early pioneers of biofeedback training (e.g., Budzynski, Stoyva & Peffer, 1977), emphasized that criteria to demonstrate significant learning need to be established before any claims can be made about the treatment effect, or before the treatment effect can be correlated with biofeedback training. A criterion may be the magnitude of the psychophysiological changes that occur in the process of learning, the voluntary control over the psychophysiological responses associated with mental changes, or any other overt behaviors which can be observed. For some reason, however, this simple logic appears to have been missed in many biofeedback training research studies. Often learners are trained over a predetermined number of sessions and then the study is terminated regardless of whether or not the subjects have mastered the technique of self-regulation of the variable being studied. If psychophysiological processes are not different from those recorded from the control group, conclusions are negative (Shellenberger & Green, 1986).

Steiner and Dince (1981) assert that the use of a fixed number of trials is not appropriate when dealing with learning a task because of the variation in the rate at which different individuals learn and master the technique. Steiner and Dince further suggest that a more appropriate model would be to train the subjects to criterion, using as many trials as are required, and then continue training for a fixed number of trials until overlearning has been achieved. Although Kewman and Roberts (1983) agree with Steiner and Dince that administration of training does not necessarily equal subjects learning to criterion (a logical and common criticism of many "unsuccessful" biofeedback studies), they suggest "there is no experimentally validated training criterion for most biofeedback techniques" (Kewman & Roberts, 1983, p. 492). It is clear that further research needs to be conducted to determine both the length of training programs and appropriate training criteria (Petruzzello et al., 1991). These limitations could perhaps be overcome by a more scientific approach whereby the subjects are trained to a point of substantial symptom alteration then, through an analysis of training data, the necessary training criteria are determined for particular symptoms. Another option could be to train adequately subjects in self-regulation skills and only then to draw conclusions about the efficacy of biofeedback training for symptom alteration through self-regulation (Shellenbeger & Green, 1986). With reference to sport and exercise domains, Petruzzello et al. (1991) propose that optimal levels for the psychophysiological variables of interest need to be determined with respect to performance. They suggest that this could be done by obtaining a basic descriptive analysis of the targeted sport activity, where highly skilled subjects are then monitored during performance.

Homework Sessions

Biofeedback researchers rarely require the learner to practice via biofeedback outside the testing environment. Of the 300+ research studies on EMG, thermal, heart rate, blood pressure, and GSR feedback training reviewed by Shellenberger and Green (1986), only about 15% were found that recommended homework practice. This may be due to the underlying belief that in research, any variable outside of the testing environment (which includes homework) that affects the outcome of the intervention will invalidate the results and therefore must be eliminated. Shellenberger and Green (1986) declare that failing to provide the learner with homework exercises with or without a biofeedback instrument has hindered the development of biofeedback training. Skilled athletes can only achieve competence with regular practise. Similarly, one needs to practise regularly in order to learn to self-regulate specific psychophysiological processes. In many cases, the amount of biofeedback training done within the testing environment is insufficient for the learning of self-regulation skills and for the transfer of training to occur. This being the case, giving the learner homework should be an integral part of biofeedback training if the latter is to be successful (Shellenberger & Green, 1986).

Internal Locus of Control

In biofeedback training, the individual takes an active role in using the appropriate feedback to control the biological process voluntarily. Thus, in the reality of biofeedback training, the power to control the psychophysiological response does not come from the instrument, nor from the information emitted from the instrument. It is the learner who has the power to use the information (or to reject it, for that matter), learn the desired response, and thereafter control that response. Thus, it is the learner, not the instrument, that initiates or changes the behavior.

When the participant believes that physiological changes are controlled externally, one would expect that under experimentally controlled conditions physiological changes will not occur as expected. The strength of the belief that such changes occur only consciously and intentionally should be examined in any study which utilizes biofeedback techniques. For example, in applying the idea of an external locus of control to running, it would be the same as assuming that the runner's behavior is controlled by a stopwatch (Shellenberger & Green, 1986).

A related issue that needs to be considered is that of motivation.

Motivation

The level of the individual's motivation to gain control over his/her psychophysiological processes needs to be considered when selecting subjects for research and when developing a research design (Carlson, 1987; Shellenberger & Green, 1986). If the individual lacks the motivation to engage in change, biofeedback training will be ineffective since the efficacy of such a technique ultimately lies within the individual (Ancoli & Kamiya, 1978). For this reason, the extent to which the individual is motivated to alter his/her psychophysiological responses is a potential confounding variable that should not be neglected. The potential influence that an individual's level of motivation may have on biofeedback research outcomes led Ancoli and Kamiya to suggest that researchers should document (a) the exact manner of participant recruitment, including the selected individual's motive for participation and the criteria for rejection of other individuals; and (b) the individual's previous experience and knowledge of biofeedback. This information could aid in better understanding of biofeedback research findings and in fostering the efficacy of such a technique.

Associated with the concept of motivation is the individual's perceived competence and expectancy of success during the intervention involving biofeedback. This issue is discussed below, in relation to cognitive support provided by way of rationales, coaching, and instructions.

Cognitive Support

Failure on the part of the participant to be motivated and maximize his/her internal locus of control could possibly be a result of the researcher's failing to provide adequate cognitive support for the participant in the way of rationales, coaching, and comprehensive instructions (Shellenberger & Green, 1986). In situations where such cognitive support is not provided and the individual still attempts to utilize biofeedback information in an attempt to gain self-regulatory control, the only way the individual can learn to do this is through trial and error—an often ineffective method, particularly when there are time constraints. In human performance training such as sports, athletes are not expected to learn a skill solely by trial and error. In fact, research in sport, not to mention in psychology and education, has demonstrated the importance of a positive interaction and constructive communication between coach and athlete, therapist and client, or teacher and student (e.g., Kindsvatter, Wilem, & Ishler, 1996; Martens, 1987; Petitpas, 1996). According to Blumenstein et al. (1997), "without awareness of the program's relevance and without confidence in the program, positive change cannot take place" (p. 451). Similarly, with biofeedback it is crucial that the individual understands the feedback response, and the direction of the response, as well as having an awareness of the relationship between the response and alleviation of the symptoms (Steiner & Dince, 1981).

Shellenberger and Green (1986) claim that just as feedback as part of coaching, instructing, and the presentation of rationales can enhance motivation and performance in sport, so can such feedback enhance the efficacy of biofeedback training in both research and applied settings.

Rationales, instruction, and coaching have in many cases been excluded from biofeedback research methodology, possibly because it was believed that these variables would contaminate the results. For example, Furedy (1979) states: "... the evidence for informational biofeedback's efficacy has to be in the form of control conditions that show that an appreciable amount of increased control can indeed be attributed to the information supplied and not to the placebo-related effects such as motivation, self-instruction, relaxation and subject selection" (p. 206). However, according to Shellenberger and Green (1986), it is only when appropriate rationales and instruction are provided, together with psychophysiological training techniques, motivation enhancement, and home practice with or without a home biofeedback training unit, that the maximum benefits can be gained by the learner from biofeedback training.

Significant Others and Social Facilitation

In sport settings the feedback from significant others about an athlete's ability can have an effect on both the athlete's motivation and future level of performance. The same appears to be true when using biofeedback equipment to assist in mental training. Research findings have shown that positive feedback facilitates an individual's perceived competence and intrinsic motivation (Weiss & Chaumeton, 1992). Vallerand (1983) noted that positive feedback, regardless of the absolute quantity involved, enhanced athletes' perceptions of competence and intrinsic motivation compared to no informational feedback. Horn (1984a, b) and Horn and Lox (1993) have provided strong evidence that the quality of the feedback is important in the development of motivation. With reference to the link between the type of feedback provided by coaches and the resulting performance of the athletes, Horn and Lox (1993) noted that, following self-fulfilling prophecy theory, coaches' expectations about the ability of individual athletes often dictate or determine the level of achievement each athlete will ultimately reach.

A related issue is that of social facilitation. Ancoli and Kamiya (1978) have highlighted the possibiliy that social facilitation could be responsible for many of the conflicting results in biofeedback research. The mental training provider (or experimenter) may use different instructions and develop trust and confidence in the athlete which may facilitate motivation and the learning rate. Different instructions and interactions may inhibit the athlete's learning and cause attrition from further sessions. However, since experimenter–participant interactions are rarely documented in research reports, the influences of such interactions are difficult to evaluate. It is possible that experiments that have attempted to minimize such social interactions (in the interests of scientific rigor) may in fact have handicapped the individual's learning via biofeedback. According to Middaugh (1990), when questioning whether or not biofeedback works, the experimenter–subject interaction needs to be considered in interpreting the results and thinking about what the data really reveal. Research has documented that the extent to which the individual has confidence in the researcher's competence can ultimately affect the outcome of the intervention.

Relaxation–Biofeedback Comparison Groups

In several studies it was assumed that relaxation techniques used in conjunction with biofeedback would confound the results, and therefore researchers manipulated such variables separately. For example, Chesney and Shelton (1976) concluded that "relaxation training and practice rather than biofeedback are essential in the treatment of muscle contraction headaches" (p. 225). Kewman and Roberts (1983) reported that "there is uncertainty as to whether the efficacy of biofeedback exceeds that of relaxation training alone" (p. 489).

According to Shellenberger and Green (1986), studies that compared relaxation to biofeedback training stemmed from the misconception that biofeedback has a specific drug-like effect that increases or reduces the level of psychophysiological functioning independently of relaxation. However, biofeedback information is not a relaxation technique by itself. Rather, biofeedback information merely assists in teaching the individual to relax. Relaxation is the psychophysiological process that controls the emotional homeostasis and therefore it is more than biofeedback by itself that results in achieving optimal arousal and symptom alteration. To achieve certain biofeedback goals such as increased blood flow to the hands or reduced muscle tension, relaxation must therefore be learned by methods that are effective for this purpose. Relaxation can be achieved by either unsystematic or systematic methods. The belief that biofeedback has a specific drug-like effect led to the omission of instruction pertaining to relaxation, and to participants therefore attempting to relax through the unsystematic process of trial and error. On the other hand, participants given relaxation instructions learn to use a systematic relaxation technique and therefore effectively attain a relaxed state with a corresponding optimal level of physiological arousal and symptom alteration.

In light of the above, it is evident that studies that compare a biofeedback training group to a relaxation training group are actually comparing trial-and-error learning to systematic learning, which does not indicate the role of biofeedback in the mastery of mental states (Shellenberger & Green, 1986). Comparisons between groups receiving systematic relaxation training without the use of biofeedback equipment, and groups receiving biofeedback-assisted systematic relaxation training, would be far more appropriate. As Yates (1980) pointed out, as a bare minimum, any biofeedback study should include a control group that is treated in exactly the same way as the experimental group except that the control group is never given feedback by means of biofeedback equipment.

Baseline Readings

In order to evaluate performance as a result of training, the pertaining baseline measurements are essential (Ancoli & Kamiya, 1978; Yates, 1980). However, many of the earlier studies upon which the efficacy of biofeedback has been judged either did not include baselines as part of the basic methodology, or did not report the baseline readings, or used an inadequate time sample for such assessment (Ancoli & Kamiya, 1978; Kewman & Roberts, 1983). In such instances it is difficult to determine whether or not the change in psychophysiological self-regulation reported at the conclusion of the study was (a) a result of genuine learning through biofeedback training, (b) a normal fluctuation of psychophysiological state, or (c) an adaptation to the experimental or clinical situation (Shellenberger & Green, 1986). The same is said to be true of comparisons from baseline made in the absence of definite criteria and population norms. The question of whether or not the observed psychophysiological change is beyond the range of normal variation highlights a further problem that is evident in research literature: statistical versus clinical significance.

Statistical Versus Clinical Significance

As Zaichkowsky and Fuchs (1988) pointed out, many of the biofeedback studies that have been conducted in clinical as well as sport and exercise settings report on the success of biofeedback training by demonstrating that statistically significant changes in psychophysiological responses are evident in the experimental group compared to the control group. The question is, do statistically significant results provide conclusive support in favor of the effects of biofeedback training? The answer is, no. The obvious error in claiming support for the efficacy of biofeedback training through statistically significant results is that such findings are often made without well-established psychophysiological change occurring beyond the range of normal variation in the population. This being so, the findings may be statistically significant, but they are not functionally or clinically significant (Shellenberger & Green, 1986; Zaichkowsky & Fuchs, 1988). In order to be of clinical significance, the magnitude of the psychophysiological response must be such that the changed response (via self-regulation) affects the person in the desired manner (Ray, Raczynski, Rogers & Kimball, 1979). Shellenberger and Green (1986) proposed that researchers need to establish reliability scores for psychophysiological measures in order for "physiologically significant" differences to be determined.

Along with determining whether or not the observed changes in psychophysiological responses are statistically as well as clinically significant, the effect of adaptation should be considered and controlled.

Adaptation

Adaptation is change in the structure or function of an organism that allows it to reproduce and cope more effectively in its environment. When a stimulus is applied to a receptor, activation occurs (Sternbach, 1966). When a stimulus of constant strength is continuously applied to a receptor, the frequency of the action potentials in the receptor's sensory nerve decreases over time. This is known as adaptation. The time it takes for adaptation to occur following activation largely depends on the sense organ involved as well as on the environmental context. The adaptation effect has been well documented in psychophysiological research (Shellenberger & Green, 1987; Yates, 1980). According to Schweigert (1998), a researcher first needs to establish a stable baseline (i.e., a baseline measurement with relatively little variability) in order to detect a difference between baseline and intervention measurements. A stable baseline can only be obtained once the individual has adapted to the experimental or clinical situation. Yates points out that it is essential to adapt the subject to the experimental situation in all training sessions, not just the first. Shellenberger and Green (1986) noted that while some biofeedback studies have controlled for adaptation, other have not. Without considering the adaptation effect it is difficult to determine whether or not changes in psychophysiological responses are due to biofeedback training or adaptational changes, since adaptational changes emitted from an individual during assessment can be erroneously interpreted as evidence of self-regulated control of a target psychophysiological response (Kewman & Roberts, 1983).

Multifaceted Treatment Programs

The use of biofeedback as a component of a multifaceted treatment package is a contentious issue. If biofeedback is used as part of a larger intervention package (e.g., biofeedback plus relaxation and mental imagery) it becomes difficult to scientifically ascertain the extent to which biofeedback training actually affects performance (Petruzzello et al., 1991). However, in some experiments that involve biofeedback training as well as other intervention techniques it is possible that neither the biofeedback training nor the other intervention techniques will produce a main effect. Instead there will be an interaction effect such that when they operate together significant changes result (Rosenfeld, 1987). For example, on reporting on a clinical consultation with a client, Amar (1993) claimed that "no amount of biofeedback alone, without a psychotherapy component, would have achieved that result. Nor would psychotherapy, without the physiological self-regulation component, have reduced and stabilised his blood pressure" (p. 207).

In the sport and exercise domain, several studies (Blais & Vallerand, 1986; Blumenstein, Bar-Eli & Tenenbaum, 1995; Blumenstein, Breslev, Bar-Eli, Tenenbaum, & Weinstein, 1995; Daniels & Landers, 1981) have demonstrated the positive effects of biofeedback training used in conjunction with other psychological intervention techniques so as to control nonoptimal states which precede athletic competition. If in fact the effectiveness of various psychological interventions can be significantly enhanced by incorporating biofeedback and biofeedback training, then controlled observational research pertaining to these presumed interaction effects is necessary for further advancement of biofeedback research and application.

PRACTICAL IMPLICATIONS AND RECOMMENDATIONS FOR BIOFEEDBACK TRAINING

Despite the numerous limitations of the research studies testing the effectiveness of biofeedback and other interventions on athletic performance, the positive effects of biofeedback have been demonstrated consistently with a variety of skills. Taking into account these limitations, a question raised is how an athlete can incorporate biofeedback as a tool for training to control physiological indices. As with any other learning skill, an athlete needs to engage in systematic and deliberative practice to learn how to recognize information on physiological responses provided by biofeedback instrumentation, and alter these responses through personal self-regulation. Self-regulation of learning refers to cognitive, motivational, and behavioral processes that learners use to achieve peak performance (Zimmerman, 1999). Self-regulatory processes such as goal setting, strategy selection, self-instruction, self-monitoring, self-evaluation, and adaptive help seeking are essential in preparing athletes to engage in biofeedback training effectively.

First a learner's goals emerge from previous analyses of performance conducted by the learners themselves or with the assistance of a coach. Various specific task strategies are selected to accomplish these goals. For example, a rifle shooter experiencing tremors due to overwhelming anxiety may decide to incorporate biofeedback and mental imagery to achieve the goal to hold the arm steady and follow through. However, depending on the shooters' skill level (e.g., novice, intermediate, or expert), and past experience (having or not having been exposed to biofeedback or mental imagery before), less skilled rifle shooters may need more coaching, guidance, and support, and more extensive training sessions to recognize and learn how to alter physiological responses on their own during subsequent self-directed practice. The frequency and length of training sessions as well as the training criteria should be aimed at meeting the shooter's particular learning characteristics. Practice of the biofeedback technique should continue until automaticity is achieved. Homework exercises assigned to the athlete are aimed at practicing on his or her own to achieve mastery.

Key motivational beliefs during biofeedback training also influence an individual's motivation to initiate actions based primarily on previous mastery performances. Self-efficacy (the degree to which one believes that she or he can accomplish a task in a given situation), outcome expectations (beliefs about the ultimate ends of a performance), and intrinsic interest (without any tangible rewards) play a major role in this respect (Bandura, 1997). If the rifle shooter is not intrinsically motivated to use biofeedback to reduce his/her anxiety level and/or does not believe he or she can use the information obtained from the machine to alter performance, biofeedback will be ineffective. Explicit training in systematic practice and self-monitoring have been shown to be highly predictive of students' perceptions of self-efficacy (Zimmerman & Bandura, 1994), and therefore sport psychologists are expected to provide the athlete with detailed instruction and powerful strategies on how to utilize biofeedback efficiently and productively. Absence of cognitive support—a major methodological concern in biofeedback research designs—can diminish one's self-efficacy and, consequently, motivational level about eventually acquiring the skill. Recent research findings show that learners who rely on their own personal discovery methods reported low self-efficacy perceptions, less intrinsic interest in the task, and attributed their deficiencies to external, uncontrollable sources (e.g., ability, and lack of sufficient effort). In contrast, learners who received social guidance during the initial levels of learning complex cognitive skills made more attributions to strategy deficiency, reported high self-efficacy perceptions, more satisfactory self-reactions, and greater intrinsic motivation to pursue the skill further (Zimmerman & Kitsantas, 1996; 1997; 1999; Kitsantas & Zimmerman, 1998; Kitsantas, Zimmerman, & Clearly, in press). Therefore, comprehensive instructional models (e.g., Blumenstein et al., 1997) should be made available to athletes to prepare them for competition.

During performance of the biofeedback technique, self-monitoring could play a critical role in the learning process. Self-monitoring refers to deliberate attention to some aspect of one's behavior (Kanfer, 1971). Self-monitoring requires learners to attend selectively to specific actions and cognitive processes. Following display of information about the state of selected physiological functions, the rifle shooter may use self-monitoring to observe and keep track of his/her own performance and outcomes. Self-monitoring of processing errors draws the learners' attention to motoric components that need to be corrected. The rifle shooter may also self-instruct and keep records while self-observing his or her performance in an effort to determine the triggers of involuntary responses following practice. These records assist the athlete in modifying strategy as areas of deficiency are mastered and adjusting his/her goals during the next practice cycle. In short, instructors are recommended to teach their athletes to self-monitor during biofeedback training in order to help them become aware of their initial shortcomings in biofeedback usage.

Finally, self-evaluating performance to prepare the athlete for the next course of action is of utmost importance. Self-evaluation refers to judgments of performance according to a standard (Kanfer, 1971). The person's self-reactions and attributions may have an effect on his/her motivational level. For example, self-reactions such as self-satisfaction and positive affect, and attributions for failure to strategy deficiency, lead to greater motivation and self-efficacy beliefs to sustain efforts on the task (Zimmerman & Kitsantas, 1997; 1999). Continuing with our example, the rifle shooter now attempts to evaluate (based on self-monitored information) the effectiveness of biofeedback in combination with mental imagery to control his/her anxiety level and his/her success in achieving the process goal. He or she can analyze the biofeedback records obtained while performing the task. If the athlete encounters difficulty in analyzing these records, social assistance should be sought for further analysis, discussion, and feedback. The athlete's satisfaction or dissatisfaction with his/her performance affects the motivation, goal setting, planning, and strategy selection in the next cycle of practice. Additionally, the athlete may seek to test different biofeedback modalities, such as desensitization, music, and relaxation, in an effort to determine what works best.

Biofeedback training requires more than obtaining information through appropriate instruments. It requires systematic instruction, social guidance, and use of self-regulatory processes in selecting appropriate biofeedback modalities and mental techniques, and evaluating outcomes until the skill becomes automatized. Once the skill is mastered, athletes can independently alter their arousal states and effectively deal with adverse conditions during competition.

FUTURE DIRECTIONS AND CONCLUSIONS

Methodological Aspects

To advance the methodology associated with the use and experimentation of biofeedback, a substantial number of variables should be taken into consideration. We summarize the previously discussed concerns within an integrative framework shown in Figure 6.1.

There are several sources of "noise" in research into the use of mental techniques that incorporate biofeedback devices. The first one is the participant. The first of the participant's main features that deserves attention is the participant's past experience with any kind of mental technique, whether practiced with or without physiological feedback. Secondly, the degree to which the person is motivated to practise the mental techniques and biofeedback until he/she experiences some control over the mental state is also important. However, the most crucial aspect is the extent to which the participant is willing to adopt the technique. Lack of motivation may jeopardize any attempt to learn the technique and control the mind, emotions, and mental state of the learner. As far as we know, personal variables have not been taken into consideration in biofeedback research, and therefore we lack empirical evidence as to the personal characteristics required to increase the openness towards developing an optimal mental state when trained with biofeedback.

Another crucial variable, which may be viewed as a moderator or intervening variable between the person and the outcome, is the quality of the instruction (i.e., coaching) given to the learner. Educational research shows that quality of instruction is strongly and linearly related to learning outcome (see Bloom, 1976 for a review). There is no reason to believe that this is not true for the learning of mental techniques that result in better control over one's mental and emotional state.

To account for the effect of quality of instruction, an operational definition of the variables that comprise it is necessary. Cognitive support and social facilitation can be seen as reinforcers and motivators of engagement and adherence to the learning process. However, the precise instructions and guidance needed are not so clear.

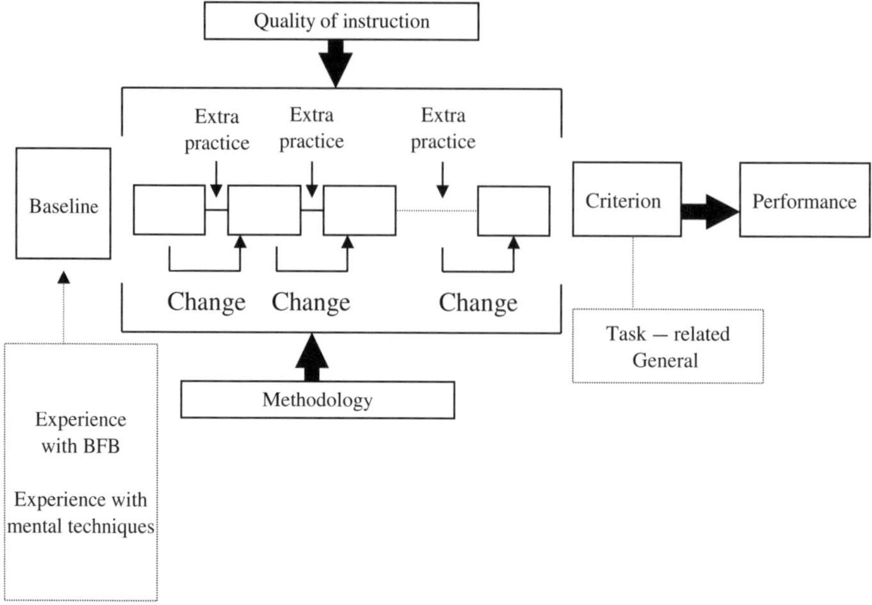

Figure 6.1 A model summarizing the main variables of concern in the study of mental techniques incorporating biofeedback. Definitions: *Quality of instruction:* cognitive support, guidance (rationales, instructions, coaching); Social facilitation; experimenter (coach)–participant interaction. *Extra practice:* how much, nature, with/without biofeedback, with/without mental technique, conditions controlled? *Methodology:* number of trials, duration of trials, interval length, experimental vs. control (biofeedback, biofeedback + mental technique, control), feedback mode, equipment used. *Change:* statistical vs. clinical importance; adoption rate

Specific instructions associated with the learning of relaxation and excitation are well known and documented, but instructions that facilitate control over physiological indices should be further studied and developed.

An additional component viewed as vital to the study and application of mental techniques incorporating biofeedback is the soundness of the methodology. The length of time, the number of trials and their duration, and the physiological mode (HR, GSR, VO_2, EMG, EEG, etc.) under which the mental techniques are provided and practiced should be held constant across repeated studies. Only results of repeated studies that share identical procedures can later be generalized. Too many methodological variations in the study of biofeedback have resulted in equivocal and inconsistent results.

Related to these methodological issues are additional variables with effects on outcomes that have to be taken into account. The first is the equipment and devices used for biofeedback, including the physiological modality with which the participant practices the mental technique. Researchers have tended to assume that all devices are equally sensitive and share similar physiological output. We are not certain that this is the case, as the majority of the studies have failed to test this assertion. Secondly, control over the "nature of practice" that participants undergo is lacking. This may be a crucial variable, which may determine the learner's adaptability and control over his/her mental and emotional state.

Finally, definitions of the terms "criterion," "change," and "criterion–performance linkage" have to be established. Anyone who uses biofeedback equipment realizes that physiological alterations occur with alteration of mental and emotional states. However, the determination of a sufficient or acceptable alteration remains vague and unclear. For example, is the criterion limited to one physiological mode? Is it task-specific or task-independent? So long as the criterion remains undefined, the evaluation of physiological changes associated with mood, emotions, and/or feelings will remain unclear. Furthermore, the effect of these changes on performance variables cannot be determined with confidence.

We do not claim that all sources of variation can be controlled and explained experimentally. Anecdotal evidence and the experiences of practitioners are also a source of scientific knowledge. The issue of biofeedback, which may supplement the research findings, has lost its momentum, partially because of the lack of progress in scientific knowledge of the issue. The introduction of new technologies such as magnetic resonance imaging may revive this field of inquiry, but methodological concerns should be addressed so that the role of biofeedback in the treatment and mental preparation of athletes can be specifically documented.

Practical Aspects

Taking into account the distinctive experiences that athletes undergo and the various unique situational variables, it is a challenge to develop and empirically test the effectiveness of a specific training biofeedback regime in conjunction with other mental techniques for athletes. A comprehensive model of mental training with biofeedback, the "Five-Step Approach" by Blumenstein et al. (1997), also presented in Chapter 4 of the present book, provides a detailed description for practitioners incorporating biofeedback training. This five-step mental preparation model consists of five stages each with a substantial number of sessions and increasing in difficulty and complexity to help the athlete achieve optimal arousal control. This model takes into consideration the methodological concerns mentioned earlier and therefore enhances the quality of athletes' self-directed practice episodes and sustains their motivation to use and adhere to its procedures. Training in the use of specific self-regulatory processes for athletes within this conceptual framework is presented in Figure 6.2.

Stages 1 and 2 in the model of Blumenstein et al. (1997) requires the athletes to use specific instruction and demonstrations on biofeedback techniques and modalities. Practitioners are encouraged to assist learners in adapting process goals that are hierarchically linked to outcome goals. "Process goals" refer to methods and strategies that can help athletes to master a task, whereas "outcome goals" specify the outcomes of learning efforts. Process goals are advantageous because they focus the learner's attention on specific components of the task (Zimmerman, 1999). Outcome

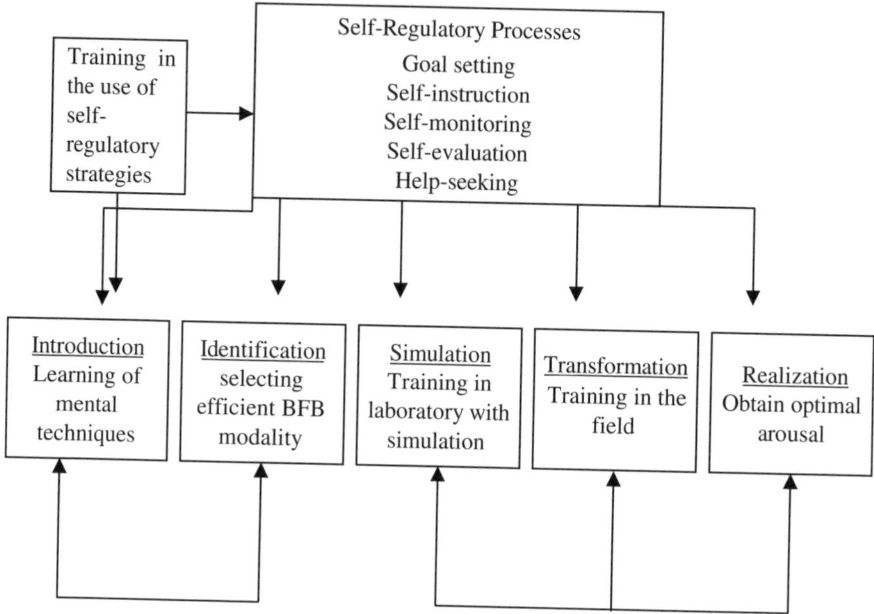

Figure 6.2 Self-regulated processes within the "Five-Step Approach" introduced by Blumenstein, Bar-Eli, and Tenenbaum (1997). Reproduced by permission

goals assist learners later in the learning process, when they adapt their automatized performance skills to competitive naturalistic conditions (realization stage) (Zimmerman & Kitsantas, 1999). Young and novice athletes engaging in mental practice should first acquire the mental techniques in order to control their arousal level. Concentrating on arousal levels before achieving mastery of a mental technique can interfere with an athlete's goal of routinizing process components and lead to negative self-reactive forms such as dissatisfaction with one's own competence. Thus, selecting and mastering specific biofeedback techniques before concentrating on achieving optimal control of arousal levels is critical.

Second, instructors are recommended to teach their athletes to self-monitor during practice. Self-monitoring can be enhanced by keeping records particularly during the simulation and transformation stages of learning. Keeping track of whether all steps of the imagery technique were followed during training with simulated competitive stress reduces an athlete's need for recall, and leads to enhanced control of the mental performance. In addition, after automatization is achieved athletes can shift their attention from process to outcome goals and concentrate on monitoring their arousal level (transformation and realization stages). During practice episodes athletes can also self-instruct themselves. Overt or subvocal verbalizations can guide and motivate athletes' performance.

Third, following completion of the practice or competitive sessions, instructors should encourage their athletes to self-reflect on their performance, whether in a laboratory or field setting. Self-evaluation results in alterations of mental strategies and adjustment of mental techniques based on self-monitored feedback (Kitsantas & Zimmerman, 1998). Self-evaluation may be implemented behaviorally in the form of self-recording. During independent practice of mental techniques, athletes can use these tangible performance records to identify and subsequently correct errors in their performance on their own. Adaptive help seeking should be encouraged when the athlete does not know how to correct a flow in his or her performance. Hence, selecting biofeedback modalities and mental techniques requires more than systematic instruction; it requires personal self-regulation particularly during self-directed practice.

Most of the methodological problems identified and discussed in this chapter (cognitive support, training criteria, motivational processes of the athlete, social facilitation, and homework sessions), may be difficult to control due to individual differences and the unique needs and experiences of each athlete. Case study designs and more individualized biofeedback packages with training in self-regulatory processes may provide the means for capturing and documenting the significant contributions of biofeedback in mental preparation of athletes.

CONCLUDING SUMMARY

Biofeedback is a technique that enables people to develop self-control over their mental and emotional states. The final aim is to enhance performance through the use of optimal self-regulatory mechanisms that have been found to affect directly behaviors that are highly associated with optimal functionality. Biofeedback incorporating mental techniques for relaxation–excitation mode control with its modalities and applications in sport and exercise became one of the most promising areas for research and applications. This chapter pointed out the concerns that the practitioner and the scientist should take into account when practicing and researching the processes and outcomes of mental techniques with biofeedback devices. Once these concerns are appropriately taken into account, both the scientific and practical outcomes are sound and can be repeated.

In this chapter a distinction was made between the terms "biofeedback" and "biofeedback training." The biofeedback hardware is conceptually distinguished from the mental techniques that are employed in various settings and are aimed at facilitating learning and self-regulatory mechanisms of arousal–emotional–mental control. As inherited problems in the biofeedback training, several methodological limitations were outlined that practitioners and scientists should take into account when applying biofeedback in their practice and/or research.

The practical implications for biofeedback training were also outlined. Such training is aimed at self-regulatory processes such as goal setting, strategy selection, self-instruction, self-monitoring, self-evaluation, and adaptive self-seeking. The role that self-efficacy and motivation play in acquiring proficient mental and emotional skills while learning self-regulation through the assistance of biofeedback was emphasized.

Social guidance and support, mainly during the initial stages of biofeedback learning, is of primary importance. Systematic instruction, social guidance, and self-regulatory processes when appropriately applied secure successful application of biofeedback.

New directions were offered in biofeedback research and applications. The chapter recommended a sound methodological framework that relies on scientific, anecdotal, and practical sources of evidence to advance theoretical conceptions of biofeedback training. Finally, it also outlined what practitioners and researchers should do to ensure desirable mental strategy adjustments.

REFERENCES

Ancoli, S., & Kamiya, J. (1978). Methodological issues in alpha biofeedback training. *Biofeedback and Self-Regulation*, **3**, 159–183.

Amar, P. B. (1993). Biofeedback and applied psychophysiology at the crossroads. *Biofeedback and Self-Regulation*, **18**, 201–209.

Ash, M. J., & Zellner, R. D. (1978). Speculations on the use of biofeedback training in sport psychology. In D. M. Landers & R. W. Christina (eds.), *Psychology of motor behavior and sport*. Champaign, IL: Human Kinetics.

Bandura (1997). *Self-efficacy: The exercise of control*. New York: W.H. Freeman.

Blais, M., & Vallerand, R. (1986). Multimodal effects of electromyographic biofeedback: Looking at children's ability to control precompetitive anxiety. *Journal of Sport Psychology*, **8**, 283–303.

Blanchard, E., Adrasik, F., & Silver, B. (1980). Biofeedback and relaxation in the treatment of tension headaches: A reply to Belar. *Journal of Behavioral Medicine*, **3**, 227–231.

Bloom, B. S. (1976). *Human characteristics and school learning*. New York: McGraw-Hill.

Blumenstein, B., Bar-Eli, M., & Tenenbaum, G. (1995). The augmenting role of biofeedback: Effects of autogenic training, imagery and music training on physiological indices and athletic performance. *Journal of Sport Sciences*, **13**, 343–354.

Blumenstein, B., Bar-Eli, M., & Tenenbaum, G. (1997). A five step approach to mental training incorporating biofeedback. *The Sport Psychologist*, **11**, 440–453.

Blumenstein, B., Breslev, I., Bar-Eli, M., Tenenbaum, G., & Weinstein, Y. (1995). Regulation of mental states and biofeedback techniques: Effects on breathing pattern. *Biofeedback and self-regulation*, **20**, 169–183.

Boutcher, S. H., & Zinsser, N. W. (1990). Cardiac deceleration of elite and beginning golfers during putting. *Journal of Sport and Exercise Psychology*, **12**, 37–47.

Budzynski, T., Stoyva, J., & Peffer, K. (1977). Biofeedback techniques in psychosomatic disorders. In E. Foa & A. Goldstein (eds.), *Handbook of behavioral interventions*. New York: John Wiley & Sons.

Carlson, G. C. (1987). Comments of the Furedy/Shellenberger-Green debate. *Biofeedback and Self-Regulation*, **12**, 223–226.

Chesney, M., & Shelton, J. (1976). A comparison of muscle relaxation and electromyogram biofeedback treatments for muscle contraction headache. *Journal of Behavior Therapy and Experimental Psychiatry*, **7**, 221–225.

Collins, D. (1995). Psychophysiology and sport performance. In S.J.H. Biddle (ed.), *European perspectives on exercise and sport psychology* (pp. 154–178). Leeds, UK: Human Kinetics.

Daniels, F. S., & Landers, D. M. (1981). Biofeedback and shooting performance: A test of disregulation and systems theory. *Journal of Sport Psychology*, **4**, 271–282.

De Witt, D. J. (1980). Cognitive and biofeedback training for stress reduction with university athletes. *Journal of Sport Psychology*, **2**, 288–294.

Engle, B. T., & Bailey, W. F. (1983). Behavioral applications in the treatment of patients with cardiovascular disorders. In J.V. Basmajian (ed.), *Principles and practice for clinicians* (2nd ed.). (pp. 228–238) Baltimore: Williams & Wilkins.

Fischer-Williams, M., Nigl, A. J., & Sovine, D. L. (1981). *A textbook of biological feedback*. New York: Human Sciences Press.

Furedy, J. J. (1979). Teaching self-regulation of cardiac function through imaginational pavlovian and biofeedback conditioning: Remember the response. In N. Birbaumer & H. Kimmel (eds.), *Biofeedback and self-regulation* (pp. 205–225). New York: John Wiley & Sons.

Hackfort, D., & Schwenkmezger, P. (1993). Anxiety. In R. N. Singer, M. Murphey, & L. K. Tennant (eds.), *Handbook of research on sport psychology* (pp. 328–364). New York: Macmillan.

Heil, J., & Henschen, K. (1996). Assessment in sport and exercise psychology. In J. L. Van Raalte & B.W. Brewer (eds.), *Exploring sport and exercise psychology* (pp. 229–255). Washington, DC: American Psychological Association.

Heibloem, P. H. (1990). *Alpha mind power training*. Nambour, Queensland: P. H. & C. F. Heibloem.

Horn, T. S. (1984a). Expectancy effects in the interscholastic setting: Methodological considerations. *Journal of Sport Psychology*, **6**, 60–76.

Horn, T. S. (1984b). The expectancy process: Causes and consequences. In W. F. Straub and J. M. Williams (eds.), *Cognitive sport psychology* (pp. 199–211). Lansing, NY: Sport Sciences Associates.

Horn, T. S., & Lox, C. (1993). The self-fulfilling prophecy theory: When coaches expectations become reality. In J. M. Williams (ed.), *Applied sport psychology: Personal growth to peak performance* (2nd ed.). London: Mayfield Publishing Company.

Kanfer, F. H. (1971). The maintenance of behavior by self-generated stimuli and reinforcement. In A. Jacobs & L.B. Sachs (eds.), *The psychology of private events* (pp. 398–416). New York: Academic Press.

Kewman, D. G., & Roberts, A. H. (1983). An alternative perspective on biofeedback efficacy studies: A reply to Steiner and Dince. *Biofeedback and Self-Regulation*, **8**, 487–497.

Kamiya, J. (1968). Conscious control of brainwaves. *Psychology Today*, **1**, 57–60.

Kindsvatter, R., Wilem, W., & Ishler, M. (1996). *Dynamics of effective teaching* (3rd ed.). New York: Longman.

Kitsantas, A. & Zimmerman, B. J. (1998). Self-regulation of motoric learning: A strategic cycle view. *Journal of Applied Sport Psychology*, **10**, 220–239.

Kitsantas, A., Zimmerman, B. J., & Clearly, T. (in press). The role of observation and emulation in the development of athletic self-regulation. *Journal of Educational Psychology.*

Martens, R. (1987). *Coaches' guide to sport psychology*. Champaign, IL.: Human Kinetics.

Middaugh, S. J. (1990). On clinical efficacy: Why biofeedback does—and does not—work. *Biofeedback and Self-Regulation*, **15**, 191–208.

Miller, N. E. (1969). Learning of visceral and glandular responses. *Science*, **163**, 435–435.

Murphy, S. M., & Woolfolk, R. L. (1987). The effects of cognitive interventions on competitive anxiety and performance on a fine motor skill accuracy task. *International Journal of Sport Psychology*, **18**, 152–166.

Nowlis, D. P., & Kamiya, J. (1970). The control of electroencephalographic alpha rhythms through auditory feedback and the associated mental activity. *Psychophysiology*, **6**, 476–484.

Petitpas, A. J. (1996). Counselling interventions in applied sport psychology. In J. L. Van Raalte, & B. W. Brewer (eds.), *Exploring sport and exercise psychology.* Washington, DC: American Psychological Association.

Petruzzello, S. J., Landers, D. M., & Salazar, W. (1991). Biofeedback and sport/exercise performance: Applications and limitations. *Behavior Therapy*, **22**, 397–392.

Ray, W. S., Raczynski, J. M., Rogers, T., & Kimball, W. H. (1979). *Evaluation of clinical biofeedback.* New York: Plenum Press.

Rosenfeld, J. P. (1987). Can clinical biofeedback be scientifically validated? A follow-up on the Green-Shellenberger-Furedy-Roberts debates. *Biofeedback and Self-Regulation*, **12**, 217–222.

Sandweiss, J. H., & Wolf, S. L. (1985). *Biofeedback and sport science*. New York : Plenum.

Schweigert, W. A. (1998). *Research methods in psychology: A handbook.* Melbourne: Brooks/Cole.

Shellenberger, R., & Green, J. A. (1986). *From the ghost in the box to successful biofeedback training.* Greeley, CO: Health Psychology Publications.

Shellenberger, R., & Green, J. A. (1987). Specific effects and biofeedback versus biofeedback-assisted self-regulation training. *Biofeedback and Self-Regulation*, **12**, 185–209.

Steiner, S., & Dince, W. (1981). Biofeedback efficacy studies: A critique of critiques. *Biofeedback and Self-Regulation*, **6**, 275–288.

Steiner, S., & Dince, W. (1983). A reply to the nature of biofeedback efficacy studies. *Biofeedback and Self-Regulation*, **7**, 499–504.

Sternbach, R. A. (1966). *Principles of psychophysiology*. New York: Academic Press.

Vallerand, R. J. (1983). The effect of differential amounts of positive verbal feedback on the intrinsic motivation of male hockey players. *Journal of Sport Psychology*, **5**, 100–107.

Weiss, M. R., & Chaumeton, N. (1992). Motivational orientations in sport. In T.S. Horn (ed.). *Advances in sport psychology* (pp. 61–99). Champaign, IL.: Human Kinetics.

Wolf, S. L. (1983). Neurophysiological factors in electromyographic feedback for neuromotor disorders. In J. V. Basmajian (ed.), *Biofeedback: Principles and practice for clinicians* (pp. 5–22). Baltimore: Williams & Wilkins.

Yates, A. J. (1980). *Biofeedback and the modification of behavior.* New York: Plenum.

Zaichkowsky, L. D. (1975). Combating stress: What about relaxation training and biofeedback? *Mouvement*, **1**, 309–312.

Zaichkowsky, L. D., & Fuchs, C. Z. (1988). Biofeedback applications in exercise and athletic performance. *Exercise and Sport Sciences Review*, **16**, 381–421.

Zaichkowsky, L. D., & Fuchs, C. Z. (1989). Biofeedback-assisted self-regulation for stress management in sports. In D. Hackfort & C. D. Spielberger (eds.), *Anxiety in sports: An international perspective* (pp. 235–245). New York: Hemisphere Publishing Corporation.

Zaichkowsky, L .D., & Takenaka, K. (1993). Optimising arousal level. In R. N. Singer, M. Murphey, & L.K. Tennant (eds.), *Handbook of research on sport psychology* (pp. 328–364). New York: Macmillan.

Zimmerman B. J. (1999). Attaining self-regulation: A social cognitive perspective. In M. Boekaerts, P. Pintrich, & M. Seidner (eds.), *Self-Regulation Theory, Research and Applications*. Orlando, FL: Academic Press.

Zimmerman, B. J., & Bandura, A. (1994). Impact of self-regulatory influences on writing course attainment. *American Educational Research Journal, 31*, 845–862.

Zimmerman, B. J., & Kitsantas, A. (1996). Self-regulated learning of a motoric skill: The role of goal-setting and self-monitoring. *Journal of Applied Sport Psychology*, **8**, 60–75.

Zimmerman, B. J., & Kitsantas, A. (1997). Developmental phases in self-regulation: Shifting from process goals to outcome goals. *Journal of Educational Psychology*, **89**, 29–36.

Zimmerman, B. J., & Kitsantas, A. (1999). Acquiring writing revision skill: Shifting from process to outcome self-regulatory goals. *Journal of Educational Psychology*, **91**, 241–250.

Conclusion

In this book our international team of authors attempted to demonstrate that applied psychophysiology and, specifically, biofeedback interventions have a great potential for sport and exercise psychology.

This book further conveys the message that psychophysiology provides a very promising direction for sport/exercise psychology, in line with Hatfield and Landers' (1983) article, "Psychophysiology: a new direction for sport psychology," Collins' (1995) book chapter, "Psychophysiology and sport performance," and Hatfield and Hillman's (2001) book chapter, "The psychophysiology of sport." At the same time, biofeedback applications illustrate that psychophysiology is "the scientific study of the relationships between mental and behavioral activities and bodily events" (Surwillo, 1986, p. 3), with biofeedback acting as the creation of a new feedback loop between the body and brain to aid in self-regulation (Schwartz, 1987).

In line with these definitions, the message of this book is quite clear: the aim of biofeedback applications in sport and exercise should be to create a self-regulating (person) athlete who possesses mental skills and self-understanding ability in order to cope with competition stress and diverse life tensions.

To conclude the book, the following are some of the main priorities for future research and practice in this area:

- Further empirical research into the appropriate content and composition of psychological skills training programs.
- Development of new biofeedback devices that will be comfortable and user-friendly for athletes and patients, for both laboratory and field settings, including telemetric versions and systems of biofeedback, and perhaps internet versions.
- Further evaluation of the effects of psychological skills training with biofeedback interventions in various sports.
- Development of treatment standards and guidelines for biofeedback training in sport.

- Development of biofeedback training models for various sport disciplines and different training preparation periods (e.g., for general and specific training preparation, prestart preparation, or recovery stage after competition and after competition season).
- Development of training protocol for biofeedback interventions (session duration, session order, loads and goals; exercises with biofeedback channels in visual and auditory versions; motivation support during biofeedback training; combination of biofeedback with other psychological techniques, etc.).
- Development of biofeedback applications for rehabilitation after sport injuries.
- Development of interpretation tools and provision of useful recommendations for coaches and athletes.
- Improvement of the application of biofeedback in real life.

According to the Thorndike–Barnhart dictionary, application is “a putting to use” (p. 70). We hope that this book will be a major step in this direction, and that it will show how biofeedback can be put to use in real-life situations. All this will allow the improvement of biofeedback application in our real life.

REFERENCES

Barnhart, C. L. (ed.). (1967). Thorndike-Barnhart Dictionary. Garden City, NY: Doubleday.

Collins, D. (1995). Psychophysiology and sport performance. In S. J. Biddle (ed.), *European perspectives on exercise and sport psychology* (pp. 154–178). Human Kinetics.

Hatfield, B., & Hillman, C. (2001). The psychophysiology of sport: A mechanistic understanding of the psychology of superior performance. In R. Singer, H. Hausenblas, & C. Janelle (eds.), *Handbook of sport psychology* (pp. 362–386) (2nd ed.). New York: John Wiley & Sons.

Hatfield, B., & Landers, D. (1983). Psychophysiology—A new direction for sport psychology. *Journal of Sport Psychology*, **5**, 243–259.

Schwartz, M. S. (1987). *Biofeedback: A practitioners' guide*. New York: Guilford Press.

Surwillo, W. W. (1986). *Psychophysiology: some simple concepts and models*. Springfield, IL: Charles C. Thomas.

APPENDIX 1

Biofeedback Laboratory and Equipment

A biofeedback laboratory requires:

- A quiet room (approximately 5 × 3 m) with adjustable light intensity and black-out curtains on the windows
- A comfortable reclining chair
- Biofeedback equipment (laboratory and portable versions), TV and VCR system, musical center.

BFB equipment: In recent years, the "high-tech" industry has developed and produced different biofeedback equipment with corresponding computer program service (multimedia and graphics capability) in laboratory and portable versions. Among the more well-known ones are:

LABORATORY BIOFEEDBACK DEVICES

The I-530 System (J & J): Physiological monitoring system consists of EMG module, temperature module, respiratory module, plethysmograph module (physiological monitoring HR, blood volume pulse), EEG module. Each modality module may contain as many as four signal outputs (four channels). The I-330 system is designed for practitioners and researchers.

Neurodata EEG Physiograph: Includes two EEG channels, two conductance channels (one for temperature and one for electrodermal activity). The Neurodata EEG Physiograph is an educational and research tool for health care professionals.

ProComp$^+$ with Biograph: Includes EMG, EEG, temperature, EDR, HR, respiration, and blood volume pulse modalities. Users can work with one modality or combine any number simultaneously.

Atlas M-8600: Consists of eight-channel sensors, enabling continuous on-line monitoring of psychophysiological parameters (HR, GSR, EMG, EEG, respiratory). Selected parameters may be displaced on the monitor in a variety of graphical forms for research purposes or in various displays, such as computer games with squares, moving figures, clock, and analog to facilitate BFB training.

Ultrasis (formerly Ultramind): Relax Plus is a computerized system comprised of a biosensor infrared transmitter, PC-linked receiver, and specialized software. The system monitors changes in electrodermal activity (skin impedance changes caused by a shift in the emotional state) by means of a sophisticated sensor attached to two fingers. The software includes graph-based exercises, muscular relaxation training, mind-activated games, and multimedia animations. Training system can be used in laboratory and in field conditions.

F1000 Feedback Training System: Designed to enhance the feedback process. The F1000 includes EMG, EEG, HR, temperature, skin conductance, respiration, and tactile input.

PORTABLE BIOFEEDBACK DEVICES

Mind Master[801] *and Stress Master*[802] by Atlas: Skin response monitors, reflecting the variations in sweat gland activity. These small portable home/personal apparatuses, with the two conductive metal sensor plates, have a light pointer and sound feedback that automatically and proportionally register the level of transitory stress and diminish as transitory stress diminishes.

Biofeedback 5 DX: Microminiature surface mount technology in both sensors and monitor enhances reliability, accuracy, and compactness. All monitors have outputs for data acquisition to work with most DAC systems, and interconnects to provide tone and digital feedback for relaxation training and muscle rehabilitation in five modalities: HR, EMG, temperature, blood volume pulse and skin conductance.

MyoTrac and MyoTrac 2: Highly sensitive compact EMG monitor with built-in memory allows pre-programming of a complete training regime. May be used in the clinic, home, or office.

NeuroHarmony: Portable neurofeedback system that measures the brainwaves (EEG) from the prefrontal and both left and right hemispheres. Neurofeedback training programs (pictures, games) may be developed by connecting it with a computer and may be used in sport, education, and health.

APPENDIX 2

BIOFEEDBACK TRAINING PROTOCOL

Athlete's name: __________________ Sport discipline: __________________

Session (step) number: ________ Date: ________ Time: ________ ________
Beginning End

I. BFB modalities: HR, GSR, EMG, Temp., EEG, respiration — Schematic description of treatment sessions and marks:

Amplitude
Initial values ________
Final values ________

Type of feedback
1. Visual
2. Audio
3. Verbal

II. Training program: Mode and length of treatment — Conditions/settings: Lab–Training–Competition

1. Relaxation
2. Excitation
3. Concentration exercises
4. IM
5. Music impact
6. Breathing pattern
7. VCR

III. Conclusions and recommendations:

____

____

____

Homework:

____

____

____

Index

Index compiled by Hazel Bell